Charlotte O. Marshall

Mullings and Musings II

A Journey from Grace to Grace

Copyright 2011 © Charlotte O. Marshall
Charlotte Marshall Press
All Rights Reserved

No part of this book may be reproduced or transmitted in any form or by any means, electronic or mechanical, including photocopying, recording, or by any information storage or retrieval system, without permission in writing from the author, Charlotte O. Marshall, 2742 Chapel Hill Road, Clarksville, Tennessee 37040 or her duly authorized agent.

Unless otherwise noted, all scripture quotations are from the New Revised Standard Version Bible, copyright 1989, Division of Christian Education of the National Council of the Churches of Christ in the United States of America. Used by permission. All rights reserved.

ISBN 0970641710
EAN 978-0-9706417-1-7

Printing 10 9 8 7 6 5 4 3 2 1

Published under the auspices of *Trinity Episcopal Church*, 317 Franklin Street, Clarksville, Tennessee 37040. The proceeds from the sale of this book are to be used exclusively for the benefit of the music department of Trinity Episcopal Church and for no other purpose. Any other use will result in the reversion of all rights to the author, her heirs and assigns. This book may be purchased by contacting Trinity Episcopal Church at 931.645.2458, Monday through Friday from 9 a.m. - noon or 1 p.m. - 4 p.m.

Cover: Charlotte Marshall in red chalk and charcoal.
By Remo Triete Russo, 1951.

To my beloved daughter, Emily

Her tenacious work made this book possible.

Thank you, thank you.

CONTENTS

Preface

Acknowledgments

Mullings and Musings II

Beyond Knowing	13
Good Friends and Acquaintances: Some Here and Some There	37
Grace Abounding	65
Hellfire	77
History	83
Kirkwood	107
Mama and Daddy	125
Prophesies	139
Relatives & Acquaintances: Some Here and Some There	143
Saints	197
Sheep, Goats and Others of God's Creation	205
Unorthodoxy and Questionable Theology	237
Wars	251

PREFACE

By many requests, here is the final book of the unpublished doggerel of *Mullings and Musings*. I have grown old, as you can see, and it is my hope that some elderly wisdom is in these pages as some joyful recountings of things past. What the theme is in these writings is clear; the love we are to share with one another, a love that lives for wit as well as wisdom, and a love that will not let us go.

May God bless us, everyone.

COM

January 2011

ACKNOWLEDGMENTS

Without the help of these persons, this work would not have been possible. They are the following: Jill Hastings of *The Montgomery County Archives*; Chris Smith of *The Leaf Chronicle*; Alice Pae, my adoptive daughter; Charles Marshall, our professional publisher; Hedy Ross Russo, a source for articles and photos, and Jim Marshall, proofreader and conversationalist.

Mullings and Musings II

A Journey from Grace to Grace

BEYOND KNOWING

1

Dorothy Ann Ross Russo (1915-2009)

You have given me my deeper thirsting after life. Surely there is no greater gift to man than that which turns all his aims into thirsty lips and all life into a fountain.
The Prophet Kahlil Gibran

I first set eyes on Dorothy Ann Ross in 1939 when I was a junior at Clarksville High School and walked into her first year French class. Being seven years older than I, she had just graduated from Vanderbilt and was hired by the high school as French teacher. What a glory she was! Elegantly curved and casually dressed, she appeared with ease and confidence before our teenage eyes, and I marveled from my back row desk at this apparition of sophistication. One of her less studious students—a muscled football player—couldn't keep his eyes away. They imagined forward passes and high scores and found him hanging around the door after class.

Miss Ross began our education not only in French, but into many facets of life, which included the social graces. Life to her was indeed a fountain of knowledge, of idealism, of singing, of drama, poetry, and, yes, even dancing. Kirkwood was never like this; French class was excitement and fun. Even though we butchered every pronunciation, we sang in French. I remember yet each line of Deep Purple, Silent Night, and our shouting the militaristic French national anthem—*Le Marseillaise*. Dorothy Ann studied her junior year in France—thanks to her mother's vision of exposure—and spoke like a native. Our ignorance and youth gave her every opportunity to nurture her innate spirit of expectations and acceptance of all sorts and conditions, the sorts and conditions certainly including me.

A tea dance! What was that? Miss Ross knew. The upper story of the old Coca-Cola bottling plant on North Second Street was procured, a Saturday afternoon chosen, a record player subpoenaed, cookies baked, tea-punch brewed, and we were to dress our best. Such scary social graces and me with two left feet from my Baptist upbringing, and not knowing one jitterbug step, found me jittering against the wall. Another grace was appreciation of the arts: poetry, drama, and literature. Dropping Alec Guinness's name actually before he was a great name, we knew him from Miss Ross's love of foreign films. *Les Miserables* we knew long before it became a Broadway play, and I personally recited and properly butchered a poem—"Dans le Moulin de Mon Grandpère." Latent fountains, underground, were bubbling.

From 1940 to 1951, Dorothy Ann's and my world diverged. World War II and afterwards found us both married and with families, she with her two children, Helen (Hedy) and Galen. She had married an Italian artist, Remo Trieste Russo, who she had met at the University of Iowa. I had married the boy next door and was pregnant in 1951 with my first child, which found me often at Dr. Jack Ross's—Dorothy Ann's brother—office where she and I picked up our long-ago teacher-pupil relationship. Despite my roundness, Remo asked me to sit for a portrait, which hangs in our home to this very hour. This was our beginning again and my exposure to fountains that watered my lips and diluted my narrow piety.

Dorothy Ann Ross Russo was the first to begin the assuaging of my thirst.

Dorothy Ann and I smoked cigarettes and drank red wine during many an hour of forgiving the past, forgetting old dependences, and searching for the fountains that only know their source in a love beyond all knowing. I was "religious;" Dorothy Ann was of the spirit. Like her mother, she questioned all dogmas and accepted no pat answers. In her household, there were forever music, artistic friends, and cuisine I had never known in my world of cornbread and chess pie. I learned to eat, drink, and be more merry.

By 1958 I had three children and in 1963 I had an opportunity to go to Europe for about a month. "Go!" said Dorothy Ann. "Don't miss this." All the while relatives found me derelict in my motherly duties leaving my babies for so long. She and Remo kept my children, sent me abroad to meet my brother-in-law, Jim Marshall, in London, then on to Paris, to Zurich where Jim was posted, then by train to Rotterdam to board my husband's ship home to the States. What a fountain for a country girl.

The wider world of her visions for her friends and students goes on and on. They cannot be counted. After her death, every way I turn there is a testimony. What a difference one person can make. Legion were her gifts: teaching, promoting exchange programs, supporting all the arts around, Christian education, one of the founders of *Loaves and Fishes*, forever on the Episcopal Church's vestry, leadership in the Diocese of Middle Tennessee where she was awarded the "Bishop's Cross." Chief among her passions was the respect for all persons and she remained to her final hour a mighty voice for civil rights. She never compromised.

Victor Hugo wrote that a "great grief is a divine and terrible radiance that transfigures the wretched." Dorothy Ann knew this transfiguration from the death of her only son, Galen, at age nineteen. There must be a plane of sadness that sets one apart, one who has given up a treasure of all treasures. She walked the very bottom regions of grief. Such bereavement, no doubt, bares the soul and breaks the heart, and pours both out for others. Like Job, she saw with new eyes.

Dorothy Ann, however, was no candidate for sainthood and would rebel at the very thought. She had more questions than answers, quick judgments for injustices, more losings that she ultimately envisioned as winnings, and more wrath for wrongs done to any person—black or white, male or female, especially female. She did not forgive easily and loathed sloth and pretense. An immovable fountain of "right" was in her genes.

At 93, my counselor, my confidant, and above all, my true friend has opened the mysterious door of death and is on the other side of life. No one here has been there. But we have been assured in Holy Scripture that eye has not seen nor can anyone imagine the glory there. "Death has been swallowed up in victory." Dorothy Ann, all of us left here will "rise up and call you blessed" as you go to living waters and to strengths untold.

2

I heard the bells on Christmas Day
Their old, familiar carols play
And wild and sweet
The words repeat
Of peace on earth, good will to men
And in despair I bowed my head
"There is no peace on earth," I said;
For hate is strong
And mocks the song
Of peace on earth, good will to men...

Henry Wadsworth Longfellow

"There is no peace on earth," I said. Did not Christ himself say that he came not to bring peace, but a sword? Choose this day whose servant you must be—the sword or peace. Here is the recounting of two brothers who took vastly divergent roads:

I knew one of these brothers well—one Charles Boyd Fry (the original Jack Fry), but the other I did not know, one Sir William Fry, a Lieutenant General in the British army and upon his retirement the Governor of the Isle of Man. Both were graduates of Sandhurst, the West Point of England, but one went the way of peace, the other the way of war. Their grandfather was an Anglican minister and baptized his grandson Charles Boyd on February 25, 1860, and recorded his name in the family Bible. The present Jack Fry Marshall inherited this Bible, and it goes to our older son Charles when we are no longer here. What a repository of family history with a lock of Jim Beaumont Marshall's baby hair within its pages.

What is the story of these brothers? Thomas Hughes, the headmaster of Rugby in England, wrote a book, *Tom Brown's School Days,* that was a great success and he used his royalties to establish for the second sons of the gentry a Utopian village at Rugby, Tennessee, in the wilds of Morgan County. At 21, Jack Fry saw his escape from the military, which was against everything in his being, and joined this group of young gentlemen on this too-soon-to-fail venture. By way of Col. Killebrew, Secretary of Agriculture for Tennessee, he found his way to Rossview.

What a gentleman of peace! We would say, "laid back." As a bachelor, what contentment he found in my in-laws' home, rocking and smoking in his chair, loving every baby that came along, reading, forever reading, and having a few nips from a bottle,

Sir William Fry's home on the Isle of Man.

if one were available. His two unmarried sisters followed him here, one of whom was my husband's grandmother, Emily; and the other, Gretchen, Mrs. Alf Killebrew.

This Jack Fry was a student of history and somewhat of a prophet. He knew the roots of World War I and World War II and foretold our great conflict with Russia. He said the blessing in Latin and read French and all of us local yokels were duly impressed.

Beyond Knowing

Living to be 95, he claimed me as one of his favorites and when I sat on his bed, which was forbidden, his being an old military man, he said not one word. Jack and I were married in '47 and he died in '55. What a legacy of joy and peace he left us and how he loved our babies. In his still lovely British accent, his last words were for our 9-month-old daughter, Emily, "Let me have a peek at the little lady."

Uncle William Fry, a commander in the Cold Stream Guard, went to war—the Boer War (1899-1902) and served at length in India. The first "Bishop of Rossview," my mother-in-law, had pictures of the King and Queen of England visiting Willie on the Isle of Man, and I, myself, visited his estate there. A Masterpiece Theater setting!

What a contrast of humble contentment and powerful position for two brothers. I did not know Uncle Willie at all. He may have been a joy also, but he lived by the sword. We have a picture of him, all scarlet and sashes, ribbons and medals and rows of buttons, truly "The Lord of Man."

Who are we then? Charles Boyd, the man of peace, or William Fry, the man of empire. "Rule Britannia!" Have we become a nation of empire? "Rule Americania!" forcing our values and judgments on cultures we do not know? My soul has been joyless, muted "shocked and awed" by the cruelty of our era. After living through WWII, Korea, Vietnam, the Gulf War, and now this. "There is no peace on earth," I said. "Hate is strong and mocks the song."

Maybe I have become a Deist. God created the universe, turned man loose with his free will to see what sort of mess he could make, and the devil hasn't been disappointed. I cannot understand why, if we believe in a loving, forgiving God, we cannot hear Christ's only new commandment: "Love one another."

And remember, "God so loved the world"—not just us proper white folks with money in our pockets and good intentions, but the

Beyond Knowing

least, the outcast, the unloved. Jack Fry was the helper of the pitifully outcast—little hungry children with their father in jail.

As God hardened the heart of Pharaoh and raised up Cyrus to deliver his people, has he raised up our leaders, as some believe, to liberate the world? The literalists of John's Revelation say we are absolutely in the last times. What spirit is in control? This is my question of this so-called God of History, allowing this unending bloodshed of the innocent. I do not understand this god, nor can I pray to this god.

Last month I was in Arlington Heights, Ill., where I read the Old Testament lesson for my brother-in-law's memorial service. I read from the 24th chapter of Isaiah these words that suddenly spoke to me: "And he will destroy on this mountain the covering that is cast over all people, the veil that is spread over all nations." With Job, who am I to question the Almighty? I, bewildered and lost, say "I don't know, I don't understand, I cannot see through the veil." I will put on sackcloth and ashes. Then the bells of mystery—my not knowing and seeing through the glass darkly—begin to chime, not too loud, but cautiously chiming.

3

When Jesus saw his mother, and the disciple whom he loved standing near, he said to his mother, "Woman, behold your son!"

John 19:26

For a Mother's Day musing, the picture of the crucified Jesus, hanging in the agony of the ages, is almost too painful to contemplate; but it is one we should behold as best we can. How could any mother come to the place of her son's execution, stand there through the hours, and watch his life slowly ebb away? Jesus' words to her cry out for more explanation. They seem to say, "Mother, look at my abject helplessness—see my wounds, my rejection with spit and whip, my desertion by most of my disciples, my nakedness, and my kingdom that I proclaimed, shattered. Look at me, Mother. I am a total failure. Even God himself has forsaken me."

The veneration of Mary through the ages is testimony to her steadfast devotion to her Son even in this hour of seemingly total loss. Jesus' humanity shines forth to comfort us when he compels his mother to look at him. He knows he can no longer care for her, and he gives her into John's hands. "Behold, thy mother."

When our children are in their agonies, we as mothers and fathers must take our station at the foot of the cross. There we hear their confession of powerlessness and confusion. We are called to be faithful and stand there and wait for their death by whatever tragedy crucifies them. As we stand there, we know the ultimate victory of the cross, the resurrection and new life. We wait for the stones to be rolled away and for our children's new life of joy and purpose. Sometimes, it's a long wait, but resurrection does come—maybe not what we hoped for, but resurrection, nevertheless.

At the foot of the cross we must hear Christ's story of the Prodigal Son anew: There is no land too far, no sin too big, no squandering of resources too profligate, no dwelling with pigs too dirty that when they "come to themselves," we won't welcome them home. When the Father sees his son afar off, he runs to greet him and kisses him. Can we do any less than this? How often in our judgment we become older brothers and say, "You have just gone too far! Why don't you shape up? I don't like your friends, your dress, your hair, your lifestyle, your disregard for your elders, your chosen profession." And on and on. But in their coming home they are saying, "Behold thy son or daughter." Growing up takes a long time. Most of us are still working at it. Out of these agonies at the cross, we and our children behold each other—we parents are seen as poor fumbling mortals, prone to many judgmental and unloving mistakes; then our children are seen by us as poor fumbling mortals, trying to find their place in the world, making many unloving mistakes. We have here a mutual judgmental society.

Oh, to be like the Prodigal Son's father—to rush out in unconditional love, have a big barbecue, call in a band for the dance, and send out for jewels and new clothes. At this scene, we want our children to be like the Prodigal Son. "Behold me. I'm coming home. I've made all this mess and I'm sorry. Give me another chance. I'll do anything." Unconditional love and confession are a winning combination.

It all boils down to how we behold. Harry Truman's mother-in-law never accepted him even though he was the President of the United States—not near good enough for her Bess. So let us pray for beholding eyes that see through the sham of manmade acceptability to the truth of the love of God in Christ. All of his creation is good, and being created well, it is totally acceptable. Why do we put conditions on how to love and whom to love?

For Mother's Day, let us hear our children when they say, "Look at me." They are asking us to let them be who they are and to under gird them with the sure foundation that there's no country too far, no mistake too big that we won't be standing there at the cross. This love brings them home for resurrection. Many times when they say, "Behold thy son," we are made proud beyond our fondest hopes.

4

To me the meanest flower that blows can give
Thoughts that do often lie too deep for tears

William Wordsworth: Intimations of Immortality

Today is daffodil day for Larry. The long rows, all yellow and gold, are marching down our fence lines with such mysterious radiance that if I could understand one blossom I would know who God is and why he made Larry and me. In a white vase in front of me as I write, these daffodils seem to say—"Look at me and despair of answers. Despair of understanding the ways of the eternal in your brief time here. Despair of worthless words and try wonderment. Bask in the beauty of each petal and stamen, crafted by a hand beyond your knowing, but a hand that glorifies us daffodils and Larry and you. But remember—all are flowers of the field; we are here today and wither tomorrow."

The long rows, all yellow and gold, are marching down our fence lines with such mysterious radiance that if I could understand one blossom I would know who God is and why he made Larry and me.

Larry was the youngest son of our closest and best neighbors on Pollard Road. He was a year or two older than our oldest son, Charles, who looked up a bit to Larry because of his age and intelligence. Charles called him "Slick." Being tall, dark, and a bit reserved, he was the quiet intellectual among some of the rowdy doings of the farm boys—somehow not seeming to be cut out for farm work. "That Slick is smart" was Charles' constant evaluation; and he was, excelling in his classes, especially in math. Even though they weren't in the same year at school, these two rode the bus together, year after year, and were fast friends into young adulthood. After graduating from high school, Larry was no longer on the bus but away to college where he had some success, but suddenly too many failures. This flower of the field began to fade and has given me thoughts that "lie too deep for tears." Larry was developing schizophrenia, the most mysterious and heart-breaking of all brain diseases.

Larry's mother is one of my saints. Never once did she falter in her nurturing care of this once-brilliant son. There was never the remotest thought of his being put away from his home. Day after day, year after year, she lived with an agony of hope that there would be some treatment, some medication, some miracle to restore her son. There was nothing—nothing to impede Larry's

Beyond Knowing

deterioration and nothing to assuage the mother's loss of a son she no longer knew. This disease of the brain is creation at its cruelest.

Larry lived into his forties and died suddenly in March, 1991. During this memorial month when the daffodils bloomed, Larry's mother and I would gather great buckets of these blossoms and take them to Greenwood Cemetery for his resurrection promise. We would linger a while, speak of our years together as neighbors, remember Larry when he was his own dear, thoughtful self, and feel the full glory of spring as we sat on the sun-warmed stones.

At ninety-three, Larry's mother can no longer go to the cemetery, but today, March 23, he got his flowers. As long as I live and have daffodils and am in my right mind, the tradition shall go on. If I could understand the deepness of a mother's love, the wonder of flowers, and the joy and sadness of life, I would not have intimations but would know the immortality of Larry.

5

As the hart panteth after the water brooks, so panteth my soul after thee, O God.

Psalm 42 KJV

After World War II, when my husband was still going to sea, I often met his ship in Galveston, Texas, an island town with its own free-wheeling government. The city had a long history of gambling, rum-running, and sailor related vices. I had been warned not to appear too attractive on the streets.

Sitting alone on our hotel beach at almost sundown, I saw a solitary man in a business suit walking barefoot, shoes in hand, through the sand and surf. The month was September and the beach was deserted at this hour. As he approached I saw him looking at me and I thought—"Ah ha, one of those men out for a quick pick-up, Galveston style."

Beyond Knowing

He stopped as he came near, gave me a long look, shifted his feet in the sand and asked, "Do you know me? Have you ever seen me before?" I thought this a strange pick-up line, and I assured him I had never seen him before, that I was from out-of-town. He was fortyish, handsome, well-dressed, looking at me with sad, far-away eyes. As if on lookout, he surveyed the beach, hesitated, started again on his way, and then turned around. "Lady, can I talk to you since you don't know me and you'll never see me again?"

Since this seemed an innocent enough request and coming from a long line of talkers, I figured I could find out what his game was. His game was that he wanted a listener, an anonymous ear that couldn't tell.

He stood before me, his eyes suddenly frank and focused, and began a monologue which he was probably saying as he walked along the beach. "Lady, I am the unhappiest man in Galveston, and I can't share my true insides with anyone." He paused a moment for this statement to sink in and shuffled his feet in the sand as he continued, "In our circle, my wife and I are considered the ideal couple, the best of parents, the most dedicated church members and I, the most successful businessman in the community." Here there was an agonizing pause. "False, Lady, False! and I'm dying on the inside." Tears were near the surface as his voice lowered to a near whisper.

"My wife and I put up this smiling front with hand holding in public, but in private our hands have been known not to hold. Our children bring home honors, which are probably a result of my prodding and proud ambition for myself. My home is mortgaged to the hilt to keep up our pretenses. At church, I hold many committees together and head the funds drive, but my faith has gone with the love I once knew. My soul has dried up."

"My-wife-doesn't-understand-me" line never came. As he averted his eyes to the incoming tide, he made an allusion to some business deal that "made money and more misery." He didn't elaborate.

Beyond Knowing

When he had finished his purgation, he held me with a gentler eye, "Lady, thank you for hearing all this, and thank you for being another soul who can hear my insides. I feel better already."

My suspicions of his motives were all wrong. He only wanted someone to hear him, to share his unhappy burden. After so many years, my thoughts go back to him—probably dead by now. Did he have courage to change after his confession or was he too trapped? At least he knew the thirst that was in his soul, that he was in need of the water brooks.

Our soul's security and happiness depend on our right panting. We thirst for unconditional love, to be loved as we are, with all our mistakes, and to be forgiven for our mess-ups. This my beach confessor longed for in his marriage. For our security we long for a safe home and financial assets for our physical needs. Our hearts pant for a sense of self-worth, making us proud in our own eyes and in the eyes of our peers; but, above all, we would know a security beyond all earthly security that upholds us when all man-made efforts go awry.

If I could have replied to my friend on the beach, what would have been my words? I could not have been preachy. He had been honest with me, and he would have had to be as honest with his soul, which was truly "panting for the water brooks." That's it. We all must be honest and bare before our God. He loves us unconditionally, makes us secure, and deems us worthy sons and daughters.

> *Whoever drinks of the water that I shall give him will never thirst; the water that I shall give him will become in him a spring of water welling up to eternal life.*
>
> **John 4:14**

Beyond Knowing

6

Death, be not proud for some have called thee
Mighty and dreadful, for thou art not so.

One short sleep past, we wake eternally,
And Death shall be no more:
Death, thou shalt die.

John Donne: Holy Sonnet X

For the word "death" some prefer the euphemism "passed away," but I hear Death as the solid rock of our salvation, a good Anglo-Saxon, one-syllable word that means what it says. Christ did not pass away for our sins and John Donne did not write "Passing away, be not proud," nor Paul, "O, passing away, where is thy sting?"

With this pet peeve dealt with and with eight decades seeming to concentrate my peevishness, let me mull and muse into passing away and ponder the nearness of this passing fancy for Jack and me. Its breath, warmer and nearer, is felt as we attend more and more of these rites of passage into a place beyond our knowing—into the mystery of Death.

My husband's mother, Mary—the late Bishop of Rossview—was one of ten Beaumont children. They are all dead. Yesterday, Sunday, February 23, Joe W. Bourne III was buried at Greenwood Cemetery. Three Sundays ago, Katherine Beaumont Rudolph was interred there. On the Beaumont family tree, they were Jack's two remaining cousins in this area. Fletcher Beaumont Childs, whom some may remember, still survives in Birmingham; otherwise, Jack is the last leaf of this generation. Joe was Aunt Kitty's son; Katherine was William's daughter. William was better known as Sheriff Beaumont.

As we stood beneath one of the grand old trees at Greenwood, the melting snow clinging to its branches began to weep down upon us. It did not weep for Joe but was weeping its nurturing tears for

Beyond Knowing

the coming of spring, for resurrection, for making all things new, and perhaps for our blindness in not seeing the wonders of life and, yes, Death. The Reverend Karen Barrineau, Joe's pastor at St. Bethlehem United Methodist Church, read from the eighth chapter of Romans, words that I have long held in my inmost being as some of the most beloved of all of Paul's writings—the mystery of suffering, the promise of the redemption of the whole of creation, and the sure knowledge that nothing can separate us from the love of God.

Karen dwelt on the gifts of Grace; the Hope and Love of Joe's extended family and the Faith and fun and stories that have held them together. These gifts are the family's sure foundation and the next generation is building on these stones. Joe and Lucille have two sons—Joe IV and Wade—and an upcoming third generation of a most marvelous and diverse collection of granddaughters—one a raven-haired beauty, another a most fair blonde, and the youngest a flaming knock-your-eyes-out redhead. Lastly, there is Wade and Becky's son, Hampton, already at fifteen well over six feet tall and the heart throb of the freshman class. The family tree blossoms anew.

So, Death, what shall we say to you? Where is your sting? Death, shalt thou die? Are you truly swallowed up in victory? Hear what Isaiah says:

> *On this mountain the Lord of hosts will make for all peoples a feast of fat things, a feast of wine on the lees, of fat things full of marrow, of wine on the lees well refined. And he will destroy on this mountain the covering that is cast over all peoples, the veil that is spread over all nations. He will swallow up death forever, and the Lord God will wipe away tears from all faces, and the reproach of his people he will take away from all the earth; for the Lord has spoken.*
>
> **Isaiah 26**

7

Have you not a moist eye? A dry hand? A yellow cheek? A decreasing leg? An increasing belly? Is not your voice broken? Your wind short? Your chin double? Your wit single? And every part about you bloated with antiquity? And you yet call yourself young? Fie, fie!

Shakespeare: II Henry IV

Mr. Dick Polk called himself young. His yellow cheek was rouged, his increasing belly was corseted, his mousey hair moussed and combed over, and his decreasing leg rode high in a buggy behind a fast horse. He was longing to make a fast move on any lady acquaintance who didn't hide when he wheeled his buggy into Kirkwood society. When two unclaimed school teachers came to the community, Mr. Dick sprang into action, which included stoking the stove, dusting the erasers, filling the water cooler, and hanging around all day if it were PTA day. "Greater love hath no man!"

I can see him yet, squinting around the tin jacket of the pot-bellied stove, his gaunt cheeks a-shine from the rouge pot, clasping his old hands together again and again in anticipation of whatever his senile dreams might be. He was the laughingstock of the countryside and the bane of all women, young and not so young. Poor old fool. He died in his buggy, riding after his lost libido, a burden to himself and all around him. Fie, fie, Mr. Dick!

In contrast, Granny Ross, Dorothy Ann's mother, grappled with the reality of her years. She summed up her anguish with the succinct words: "Old age is HELL, just HELL." She refused to let the mantle of her years rest anywhere and raged bitterly at her compromised physical independence. Her mind, however, was ever independent. She doubted all cut-and-dried religious dogmas and debated all unanswerable questions which could only be answered by a leap of faith. Granny did not choose to leap. Her ever-questing mind pooh-poohed the poet Browning and his sissy lines of "Grow old along with me, the best is yet to be." She lived by the lines from Tennyson's Ulysses: "Something ere the end, some work of noble note may yet be done, not unbecoming men who strove with gods."

With these words, Granny Ross began her noble work. She was a student of Greek and Roman mythology and during her last years, she went to the public schools with many a tale of the gods and heroes. With wide-eyed wonder, the elementary students knew Ulysses, Theseus, Perseus, and the gods of Olympus. To this day, these middle-aged students recall this legacy left them by one who challenged her years and refused to yield her unique gifts of mind and spirit. At ninety-five she came to the river Styx with her existential questions still unanswered. She left us a rare example of intellectual curiosity that did not accept a cheap faith but wrestled nobly with the gods—"to strive, to seek, to find, and not to yield."

As I approach four score and eight, what shall it be for me? For us? Shall we be Mr. Dick or Granny Ross? Some of these answers are in our hands and some in the hands of our genetic make-up. We do not know our end. The scary part is that we may not be aware of our actions and responses. If our future behavior could be viewed from where we are at this moment, we would be horrified by what we have become. As we remember our relatives who have traveled this final way before us, we vow, "I shall never do that. I will never be like that." But we have no guarantees. We cannot foretell the ravages of time on body and brain. Incoherence, incontinence, and immobility may be ours. Why should I be favored not to suffer these indignities?

The loss of independence is the cruelest reality of all. This was Granny Ross's HELL. Lo, all these years we have been in control!…And here at the end of life…dependence! We will hate the ones who take our independence—our cars and checkbooks—and the hand that feeds us. As Christ said to Peter, "When you are old you will stretch out your arms, and a stranger will bind you fast and carry you where you have no wish to go." These words sound like a nursing home verdict rather than a prophesy of execution. There are times when there is no say-so in our situations. Relatives do what must be done for the good of all. What we Christians bring to these anguished times is our dependence on a mercy that is our lasting independence. We give up these unknown days to an omnipotent and omniscient love that knows no beginning or end. God rest Mr. Dick, Granny Ross, and all of us.

8

Stay me with flagons, comfort me with apples, for I am sick of Love.

Song of Solomon

It's wedding time again and I find myself mulling and musing into my repository of love quotations past.

Aunt Lucy said she didn't have any patience with love. Men weren't worth loving, children were too messy and too much trouble to love, and God was too far away to love; beside, she couldn't love anyone who created such an awful mess and then let it run itself. The worst of his mess was giving out all the lust that made these messy, bad children.

Uncle Bun, who was quite a ladies' man, assured us that love was something you could get farther behind in and caught up on quicker than anything else. No doubt he wasn't referring to the agape variety. My daddy used to say that when you were courting these pretty girls you loved them so much that you could eat them up; and after you married them, you wished you had. From my mother-in-law comes this simile quoted when she was in one of her whimsical moods:

> *Love is like a lizard*
> *It runs around your heart*
> *Then jumps at your gizzard.*

Then there are the quotes we all know: "Love is blind, it makes the world go round, it conquers all"; and then we blithely quote from the First Epistle of John the most outrageous one of all: "God is

Beyond Knowing

love." Stay me with flagons of Jack Daniel! This is a hard saying, one to skew your theological tam and leave you helpless before your pitiful understanding of such a statement.

Then I hark back to grammar school where we cut paper valentines from our OK Tablets, colored them with crayons, pierced them with long, pasted-on arrows, and wrote on the inside this innocent wisdom:

> *The river is wide*
> *And I can't step it.*
> *I love you*
> *And I can't 'hep' it.*

Somewhere beyond Aunt Lucy's cynicism, among the lizards at the gizzards, and over the wide, unsteppable river lies the great mystery—the unfathomable love that is God.

9

After rereading this 2001 New Year's edition of *Mullings and Musings*, I have set my thinking cap to wonder whether we have progressed or regressed in these five years. With old age and cynicism joining hands, I wonder at our national civility and good manners in general as traffic snarls, gas gets higher and drivers race with telephone to ear. My old VW would be lost in a forest of trucks as well as jockeying with many a distracted motorist, 80 mph and that's not the fast lane. On Peachers Mill Road, the young bloods in their pickups pass me in the middle turning lane, ignoring the traffic rules and giving me the "correct" hand sign. Young whippersnappers!

This old Jetta was finally released into the arms of a young Mennonite from Kentucky. He had advertised in a farm paper for such a car. His religious leader had made a concession that if he could find a dark colored, stick-shift, old model car, he could buy it. My husband was tired of paying insurance and license for a parked car since our grandsons had learned to drive a four-in-the-floor; this Jetta, however, had five. This was the young Mennonite's dream car. If he had gotten a brand new Jaguar he couldn't have been more pleased, and he had the $500 price tag in his pocket. These gentle people will give my faithful old friend a good home, away from the maddening crowd.

From the vantage point of 2006, I must keep faith in our humanity, made in God's image. I pray I won't turn into an "old fogey" whose handbaskets get full of doubts and grief, remembering always—"Nothing can separate us from the love of God."

> *Kind hearts are more than coronets*
> *And simple faith than Norman blood.*
>
> **Tennyson**

The New Year is here. The date 2001 doesn't seem too difficult to write, and, as the doomsdayers foretold, the new millennium hasn't found us "gone-to-hell-in-a handbasket." The sun rises as usual; the air is still breathable; our political system is intact, but slightly askew; and we find ourselves living yet in a dichotomy of faith and folly, of inhumanity and humaneness. It's the same old story. Into this cynical prologue, I, however, intersperse my story of rare kindnesses that refute all the gone-to-hell reports that grab the headlines in our newspapers. I will tell you the saga of myself, stranded on the roadside.

Home from France for July and August, our daughter had taken my car for a shopping trip when I suddenly realized I needed to go to the grocery. My husband never gets rid of his old cars and tractors—maybe that's the reason he has kept me so long—and parked out back was the '85 diesel VW I had driven until 1997. Coming to life with much gusto, the Jetta got me to the grocery, back down Fort Campbell Boulevard, onto the 101st Airborne, and into the right turning lane for Peachers Mill Road. While I was waiting for my lane to turn, there came from the bowels of the motor a shattering, grinding roar, about two coughs, and then nothing—dead, not one whirr…What shall I do?

Beyond Knowing

With a long line behind me, I could already feel road rage, bad hand signs, and curses on me and my old car. Shame on me for those ugly thoughts! I slowly got out of the car and behind me was a pickup truck whose driver was a stalwart black man. "Was he sympathetic or not?" I wondered. I remembered Fred Sanford's words—"There ain't nothing as ugly as an old white woman." I will attest here that there was no one so gracious as this young black man who pushed my clunker to the easement of the highway. All the while there was not one honk-of-a-horn in the line of waiting cars. There must have been pity for this hoary head and her poor chariot.

This was only the beginning of kindness. First, a shade tree mechanic stopped who didn't know diesel motors; then a person who knew a cheap towing service. A city Gas and Water truck driver stopped and offered his phone or to take me somewhere. An employee at the Minit Mart had already let me use his phone to call my husband. An elderly tourist who was gassing up at the pumps came over to see what I needed, declaring he would want someone to help his wife if she were in my situation. With much concern, a young woman in the store offered me an umbrella for a shade against the July sun. There was absolutely not one gesture of irritation or impatience—only kindness upon kindness. My hard, cynical heart hasn't been the same since.

We did have enough money to call B&B wrecker service whose mechanic found the timing chain—whatever that is—gone awry. The VW is fine, parked until its next adventure.

Kind hearts are indeed more than crowns. Crowns can make for tyranny, injustice, and war. Kindness is made in hearts that knows a source that transcends the selfish self and empathizes with weary fellow travelers. This kindness crowns the least brethren. I have been one on the roadside.

Simple faith is more than Norman blood, Norman blood being prideful. There is no arrogance in either kindness or faith for these are freely given gifts, ones which propel civilization upward and onward.

For a New Year's epilogue, may we be more civil each day and may we see all our brothers and sisters as beloved children of God, worthy of every courtesy and kindness. Hear what St. Paul says: "And be ye kind one to another, tenderhearted, forgiving one another, even as God for Christ's sake has forgiven you."

10

Hear what St. Paul says to the Church at Corinth:

> *Behold, I show you a mystery; we shall not all sleep, but we shall all be changed, in a moment, in the twinkling of an eye.*

"Behold, I show you a mystery"—we stand here at Neil's grave side overwhelmed with mystery—the mystery of Evil, the mystery of Suffering, and the mystery we all face—the mystery of Death. May Neil's living and dying impart to us some profound meaning in the face of the mystery of our lives on this side of eternal life. We are here so small, so unknowing, grasping for understanding as we walk the valley of the shadow of death.

We are assured that we shall fear no evil, but evil seems to have reigned. It took Neil from us. On Monday last when we gathered at the General Sessions courtroom with Ann, I looked at the young man accused of Neil's murder and wondered how he could ever come to the place of such a deed. He looked so remote, so uncaring, but unlike a person capable of such evil.

Christ in his prayer gave deliverance from evil a special supplication, "Deliver us from evil or the evil one," and Peter in his first letter to the early churches wrote—"Your adversary prowls around like a roaring lion, seeking someone to devour," and

St. Paul tells us that only by divine intervention can we be released from the scourge of the Evil One.

We know the words of this divine intervention: We do not walk the dark valley of the enemy alone. Goodness and mercy, loving kindness, and a great cloud of witnesses hold our hands and steady our feet as we walk toward the final triumph over the evil that took Neil from us.

The mystery of our suffering is as old as Adam and Eve. If God is indeed good, why do we have to imagine the pains of death that were Neil's? Why are his children, like Job, suffering unjustly? With Job's wife, we are tempted to find a vindictive way out—"let us curse God and die."

From this old Jewish play, I find a glimmer of understanding. Job was a good and innocent man who lost everything—his health, his wealth, his children, and the respect of his friends. But through the unfairness of his losses, Job came to know better who he was and his smallness in the face of the eternal. He came face to face with himself and his God.

God came on stage to question Job. In the same manner he comes to us today. "Who are you to question what you cannot know? Where were you when I spoke this mighty creation into being? Where were you when I set your home on its limestone foundation and hung the heavens with this autumn splendor? Do you know the secrets of the seasons and where the winds and rain abide? Do you know how the seeds, year after year, fill your granaries with their bounty? Can you knit together a calf in its mother's womb? Answer me this."

Here we know our finiteness, our lack of understanding and, with Job, we begin to see that suffering can bring us into a new dimension of life. Job answered God—"I had heard of thee with the hearing of my ears, and now my eye sees thee." So through our suffering we see our concept of God more clearly and we accept ourselves and others more dearly. With Job we repent in dust and ashes our lack of understanding.

Beyond Knowing

This is the gift of suffering, the gift Neil understands at last in that place where "we shall know as we have been known" and "where the glory shall be revealed in us."

Here is the greatest mystery of all: Let us hear again what St. Paul says—"We shall all be changed, in a moment, in the twinkling of an eye." His words ring out so triumphantly that we rejoice at their sound. We are going to be rid of these worn out and battered bodies. The mystery of "how" is on the other side of the glass through which we see so darkly, but we have every confidence that all creation is sacred and all things will be made new. Nothing created is every lost—it only changes its form.

Being a farmer, Neil knows what a grain of corn looks like as it dies and sends up a tall stalk above ground. Unless the seed dies, there is no new life. The death of the shriveled grain is raised up into the sunshine of a glorious harvest. One tiny seed is resurrected into a towering plant that grows from strength to strength.

Neil has been changed, in a moment, in the twinkling of an eye. The darkness of the valley of the shadow of death is lifted; the mystery of death is overpowered. "Death is swallowed up in victory."

GOOD FRIENDS AND ACQUAINTANCES: SOME HERE AND SOME THERE

11

The good must merit God's peculiar care; But who but God can tell us who they are?

Alexander Pope

We are all mysteries to ourselves and to others, and we are foolish in judgment when we say with certainty about the inner complexity of another human soul. God alone knows. Having come to this barricade, I can only project one dear to me through my eyes and my experience, and they say—"Here was a man of much more good than his outer self would ever show, a man of nameless, unremembered acts of kindness and love." God knows who he is and where he is. This personal faith lessens my grief for a lost friend.

Neil Mcphail Ross, the neighborhood's iconoclast, our eternal rebel, profane yet profound; and a friend who loved us unconditionally.

There are cruel and unfounded speculations about the mysterious disappearance of Neil Ross. These rumors, magnified and maliciously repeated, are founded in no proven facts. The only fact that is true is that Neil has gone from among us without a clue other than his abandoned truck.

Having been raised across the fence from Neil, Jack considered him almost kinfolk since the two families' interdependence went

Good Friends and Acquaintances

back several generations. Jack's usual comment about Neil was this: "He is one of my best friends and his own worst enemy." His untimely, and perhaps tragic, departure seems somehow a fated ending for his paradoxical life. He dreaded the distempers of old age and the diminishing of his powerful body. The legend of Neil will live long after him, but I cannot allow the "good to be interred with his bones."

Neil was the neighborhood's iconoclast, our eternal rebel, profane yet profound; and a friend who loved us unconditionally. We knew he was for us. He trod no middle ground—either totally for or against.

This moment I see him at our kitchen door, giving me a hug and some words of endearment and appreciation, and bringing Jack from behind his paper because <u>Neil was here</u>. There was never a lack of in-depth ideas and never any small talk or idle gossip. His brilliant mind, an encyclopedia of information and theories, kept us on tiptoes. Jack always said that he knew more about more subjects, in depth, than anyone he had ever known. His presence emanated a rare mixture of logic and irrationality, both based, however, in his wide reading and studying. With Ross genes, his mind never rested. His superlatives seemed to resonate within the "best" or the "worst"—the "best teacher" or the "worst teacher", the "kindest" friend or the "cruelest", the "wisest" or the "dumbest", the most "articulate" or the most "crude."

The second commandment is like the first. In loving your neighbor you love God. There was no "religious" good in my friend, but there was the "good" good of a big heart. Who but Neil would shelter in one of his houses a poor, illiterate woman with retardation in her family that would stun the world of abnormal psychology? Parading of piety was the target of his certain disdain. When some neighbors complained about this woman, Neil became even more loyal in his support of her. In the presence of hypocrisy, he could be most rude and crude and deliberately shocked such arrogance.

Good Friends and Acquaintances

"He who loves is born of God and knows God...for God is love." I cannot judge to what capacity my friend could love, but I do know, he loved me and my family, his family, and his dogs and cattle entrusted to him. How many tears he shed when his Standard Poodle, Gus, hanged himself in a fence and died. How often my children went to Ann and Neil when in trouble—our daughter in the depth of adolescent problems and our younger son when he was failing math. Neil's patient tutoring made him into a college bound student. One of the first professions our three-year-old, great-nephew made this year was, "I love Neil Ross." Children know.

Love of neighbor and love of animals are good indications of "what manner of man is this?" Neil tended his cattle with almost fatherly care. How many countless baby calves did he warm in the kitchen and feed on bottles when their mothers died! One of the first indications of Neil's disappearance was the bawling of the orphan calves and the lowing throughout his herd. The good shepherd was absent.

In the last years before he was taken from us, I saw my friend change. Trials, tears, and years change us all. For days he sat, uncommunicative, with feelings of failure and despair. To me he was suffering from depression, our common enemy. Untreated it can destroy and change us into persons we don't know. He came to us one night so distraught that I feared for his safety, and we sat well into the night battling with the darkness and confusion he knew.

So my friend is gone. Where he is, God knows. When he is reduced to the stuff of creation at whatever favored spot that has found him, may some great oak grow at his feet, a tangle of guarding thorns nestle him to the earth, and a wild rose crown his brow. He needs no marble to mark his place nor words of condolence said for his life. God is love and whatever portion Neil has been of this love is taken back into the unfathomable riches of Grace. That which was lost is found, is taken home with rejoicing. And the peace that passeth understanding is with us and will keep us.

12

If you lend money to any of my people with you who is poor, you shall not be to him as a creditor, and you shall not exact interest from him.

Exodus 2:3

In the winter of 1931, I was an eight year old child, and you know, children are most perceptive about the fears that go on in their household, even though unarticulated. The New Year was here January, 1932, and there was no money to pay the tax on our home or any other of our yearly accounts. My parents' solemn faces told me the worst. Neighbors were losing their homes all around. Would we be next? How much better it would have been to have shared their fears with us children, but that was not the way of my parents or any parents of that era.

Our entire economy rested on the one big cash crop: tobacco. In the winter when the markets opened and the crops sold, the farmers settled their accounts with the banks, the fertilizer and seed stores, the grocers, the courthouse and the dry goods merchants. This once-a-year payment was the norm for farmers; and most businesses were glad to "carry" these accounts if the customers were of good standing. Being of absolute good and honest standing, my parents never left a bill unpaid.

The coming of the New Year, 1932, was a different story. Tobacco prices hit an all time low with top leaf going for as little as three cents a pound. The trash *lugs* you couldn't give away. When the costs of the production for the crop was figured, there was a minus, in-the-hole, figure and there was no money for anything. Can you imagine the plight of the tenant farmer who worked for the landowners? The great depression was at its bleakest depths.

Mr. Harry Berkman and his wife, Miss Annie, owned Berkman's dry goods and ready-to-wear store, located on lower Franklin. My mother had shopped there for years and my brother vowed when

Good Friends and Acquaintances

we went to town—which was about twice a year—that he spent hours on Mr. Berkman's stools, placed there for his customers' comfort. All our yard goods, linens, underwear, hats, coats—everything except shoes—came from Mr. Berkman's well-stocked shelves and racks. Unlike our vast malls today, you found your household needs and clothing in one place and you paid your bill in January.

But alas for 1932. Mr. Berkman's kind, round face and Miss Annie's gentle demeanor and wide smile assured my parents that all was well, that they knew my parents would pay when they had the money, "Please don't worry," and "no, there would be no interest, no carrying charges." My mother gave thanks through the years for these sterling merchants. "I could not have raised my family without the Berkmans."

During World War II the Jewish community in Clarksville brought a Rabbi and his family to live here, away from the horrors of Germany. Mr. Berkman and Miss Annie brought the Rabbi and his wife and son to our home one Sunday afternoon. We did not know they were coming—a nice surprise. The Rabbi's wife played our old tiny piano and their talented son sang. Their intellect and training was obvious. There was a mutual respect between my parents and the Berkmans, else they would not have chosen to bring their new Rabbi into our modest home. How I bless the memory of these two gracious people who were not to us "as a creditor" but as friends who made us feel our worthiness when we were in need.

The Roosevelt administration began many changes and farmers' taxes were forgiven, and in many ways there was a new start. Hard times bring out the worst and the best. Sharing and forgiving were among the best.

May all follow the example of Harry and Annie Berkman, forgiving our neighbors without interest, raising them up to a sense of their worthiness, and being a creditor to no man—only debtors to God and each other for our blessings in this fair land.

13

We have all this stuff in the church to feed our need for order, yet the REAL work of the church is not to preserve order, no matter what any ecclesiastical authority figure might say. The real work of ministry takes place in the swirling mess that is life. So, get out there and get messy!

Mickey Richaud

You heard what the preacher said. Life is messy, "So get out there and get messy!" But, Mickey, you can't mean that. We were raised to be anti-messy, always smelling good, the proper gloves and hats, shined shoes, current hair styles, and for church we were doubly dutiful to proper decorum as dedicated Christians should be. And you tell us to go get messy.

Having been reared in the country it's not hard for me to make the transition from country-messer—chickens on the porch and hogs under the fence—to town propriety and proper liturgy. Then I have a town raised fellow-messer who knows about horses and mucking out stalls, who is willing for most any swirling mess. On the third Wednesdays of the month you will find Malinda Mabry-Scott and me out in the real world of *Loaves and Fishes*, serving God's forsaken and forgotten children—not by Him, but by us—as we ladle out the hash-of-the-day.

The words of a Psalmist come to me, "Though the Lord is high, yet he hath respect for the lowly; but the proud he knoweth afar off." Malinda is infectious fun with a spirit that embraces all, and she knows that there "But by the grace of God go I and the rest of us." How inclusive she is with a twinkle, a laugh, a good morning, real eye-contact, a compliment, some jovial joke, she permeates our gathering with a sense of their worth. Our two-hundred plus people of the day come alive. "Someone really sees me! Someone cares!"

Up and down the waiting line there are lively greetings and a quest for good manners. "Please" and "thank-you" abound along with admonitions to some young men to remove their hats during the

Good Friends and Acquaintances

thanksgiving, and there is help with the great stacks of trays. A happy spirit—perhaps the Holy Spirit has descended on us; and when we have finished the morning's work, refreshed and joyful, and with a merry heart, I say, "God Bless you Malinda and all Trinity's loving and caring team." When we have time to grab a bite of donated pizza, "It doesn't rest heavy on our indigestion." Merry hearts-merry stomachs.

These "Others," these ones that many consider not worthy, we find are just like us—the same pains, passions, values, hopes, fears, vanities, judgments, deceptions, and temptations. Yet some say we are giving food to the "dogs"—the woman of Canaan. Most of these hungry ones have had few crumbs from underneath life's table. The great chasm of wealth and privilege across from the one of want and poverty separates us. Again, "The Lord respects the lowly, but the proud he knows afar off."

J.W., my dear friend, has been with us for some years—a regular. His child-like simplicity and his search for the good and the right is refreshing in this day and age. He is a moralist and a judge; he confesses his frailties and his sins.

"J.W. have you ever been married?" "Nome, I ain't never been married, but I've done some shacking up, and the Lawd don't take kindly to that." His earnestness and kindness is written all over his shining face. Who among us hasn't done some shacking up? There are many ways.

One young black woman, stately and austere, the vanity of the flesh eternally haunting her, comes many days with a face marred by the most piteous rotten teeth that you can envision. With her hand over her mouth, she admits that she can get no dental care because she is only offered part time work so her employers won't have to furnish insurance. How lovely she would be if her teeth had been cared for. In winter with its cold winds, we hear—"don't give me none of that salad; my teeth hurt too bad." Yes, we have freeloaders and malingerers. There's drug abuse, alcoholism, mental illness, simple mindedness and plain laziness. We who are proud and afar off must look into ourselves and these common

Good Friends and Acquaintances

conditions we share with the lowly in this messy world. Be honest. Alcohol has ruled many in my family and drugs have butchered the finest mind among my nephews.

Malinda's inclusive soul compliments her great sense of humor, and may we learn from her the joy of acceptance. Our *Loaves and Fishes* team is a dream, and we welcome all to get out there and get messy. MAY GOD BLESS THIS MESS!

14

Here at our sea-washed, sunset gates shall stand
A mighty woman with torch, whose flame
Is the imprisoned lightning, and her name
Mother of Exiles.

The New Colossus (Statue of Liberty) Emma Lazarus

Dr. Leon Alexander

In this month's *Trumpet* under "Organ Notes" you will find this memorial gift: Dr. Leon Alexander by Mary Ann Warrick-Alexander.

Here is the story of a loyal Tennessean.

Dr. Leon Alexander, whose Polish name I do not know, fled from the Nazi eradication of Jews in his country, disguised as a chauffeur. He wandered through much of Europe, a refugee looking for escape routes, and finally found

Good Friends and Acquaintances

his way to Australia and on to San Francisco. With his first-hand knowledge of the plight of all peoples in Europe, he immediately enlisted in the United States Army, determined to help in whatever way he might be used.

He was a brilliant lawyer—one who served this country well—and after the war President Truman sent him to Europe to investigate the concentration camps in Germany and take part in the Nuremberg Trials.

As you will see from the following letter, he became most at home in Lebanon, Tennessee, and decided this was his place, his home as a naturalized citizen. He voted there and his will was probated there.

He and his wife, Mary Ann, who visits Trinity each summer, had a May – December romance; and she joined him as a partner in his Paris, France, law firm. When our daughter, who lives there, had serious legal problems, these two outstanding judicial minds were our salvation. They knew international and French law; therefore, our case prevailed in the French Courts. We owe these two our grandchildren.

Mary Ann Warrick-Alexander and her son James, pictured at right.

Good Friends and Acquaintances

I asked Mary Ann to send me some details of her husband's stay in Tennessee. Here is her reply:

Paris, 6th February, 2001

Dear Charlotte,

Thank you for your interest in Leon and his Tennessee connection. I believe that you know that Leon first came to your fine state as a Chief Warrant Officer, under requisition by the War Department in 1942, in order to study at Judge Advocates' School in Cumberland College. The system of Judge/Advocates exists in the Armed Forces in order to deal with problems of justice in times of war. This select corps consists of legal experts who act alternatively as attorney for prosecution or defense, or as judge. In Lebanon, his expertise—derived from his numerous years of experience as district attorney of the City of Warsaw, Poland, was quick to be identified, and the State of Tennessee admitted him, exempt of examination, to their Professional Bar.

Meanwhile, the U.S. Congress had passed legislation to provide compensation for war damages that would be caused by the campaign of the liberation of occupied Europe. It is of interest for Trinity Church perhaps to learn that the first compensation for war damages under the new legislation were paid to farmers in Tennessee. And Leon's first case had to do with a delicate settlement, involving just one of those cases:

In preparation for D-day in France, the War Department chose to exercise their young troops under live fire in terrain similar to the rolling hills of Normandy. Tennessee was selected as ideally suited. Hence several massive war game operations were launched, and much material damage was inflicted to farms and buildings. The farmers were then invited to file claims for damages under the new provisions of Congress. However, in case of fraud, claims were systematically disallowed.

Several farms were bombed repeatedly. Such was the case for one Tennessee farm. Examination of the claim, however, revealed a discrepancy: The same barn had been totally destroyed more than once. Leon was sent out to investigate and he found the farm to be owned by a widow. Her exaggerated claim for the destruction of her barn three times over, was hard to justify when one considered the time required to rebuild a barn. But the widow explained to Leon that she had three able-bodies sons, all of whom were serving in the Armed Forces. Whereas under regulations, Leon should have disallowed the claim entirely because of fraud, he decided to negotiate a compromise. He offered to compensate for one destruction of the barn and to bring home one of her sons to help rebuild it. However, the son would be the one of the three who was stationed closest to Tennessee, in order to be fair and spare costs to the government. Therefore it was agreed that the widow would have one of her sons (not the one she requested, but the closest) sent home and she would be given compensation for one barn.

Leon always enjoyed telling this story because it illustrated to him the proper administration of justice.

In the same way, when Leon's estate was probated in Lebanon, the judge understood that justice is not always in the application of the letter of the law, but a response to higher conscience.

For this reason, I am very pleased to associate Leon's memory to the organ at Trinity Church, because the organ is the voice of community prayer.

Love, Mary Ann

Good Friends and Acquaintances

Mary Ann attends The American Cathedral in Paris—The Episcopal Church. She and our daughter met there—two Southerners, one from Texas, one from Tennessee.

15

Anne Glass Day

Let whosoever will, come.

When I hear the name Anne Glass, I immediately smell magnolia blossoms and envision scenes from Masterpiece Theater. The Magnolias? The very essence of a South Carolina lady with Charlestonian manners and the porcelain skin of a magnolia blossom is in my mind's eye.

Masterpiece Theater? Anne's envisioned setting is an Edwardian drawing room with every inch of her coiffed and gowned as only the English bring off in their theatrical productions. As each expectant young lady performs her "piece" to a not too polite and captive room, Anne comes to the piano and WOW! Every potential beau is enraptured, every scheming mother gives a withering glance at her inept daughter, and every portly gentleman forgets his port wine and cigar.

Fantasy? Yes; but fact also. Anne's vision here is real – a vision of elegance and talent, a combination most rare, and she has been ours for forty years. She has transplanted well. Her right hand and indeed her left hand know what they are doing as well as her feet which fly, unaided by her eyes, over the bass pedals.

I marvel at her graciousness and beauty, and often there wafts across the choir an inexplicable aroma of magnolia blossoms and English lavender—*l'eau d'Anne Glass*.

Good Friends and Acquaintances

16

Oh, may I join the choir invisible of those immortal dead who live again.

The Choir Invisible-George Eliot

There is a bare spot in Trinity's choir. Israfel, who in mythology has the sweetest voice in heaven, has been joined by one of our own. In this choir invisible, newly arrived, is our *basso profundo*, Carlos Brewer. We let him go with weeping, but we rejoice and sing Hallelujah for his victories in life and his triumph over death.

Carlos and I go back some forty years. When I first knew him, he was a young doctor in Clarksville, fresh out of the army where he was a Captain in the Medical Corps. He opened his office on the corner of Fifth and Commerce Streets and began his practice there, but I knew him professionally after he moved to the Doctors' Building at the hospital.

What a wise and kind doctor he was! Being ethical in all areas of his practice, he would give you no medication unless he *ran the tests* and knew exactly what was going on in your body. There was no guesswork. Some patients wanted a cabinet full of pills, but Carlos gave only what he judged necessary and often this was aspirin and plenty of water. When you went for a physical, you knew that you had had a physical because he left you no secrets. Among his peers, he was known as the best diagnostician in town, and I personally can attest to his expertise. In 1972, I had a suspicious lump in one breast, one that a consulting surgeon had pronounced benign, but Carlos still didn't like its palpation. He ordered a biopsy, which resulted in an operation before the malignancy got into my lymphatic system. I probably owe him my life. Thank you, Carlos, for helping me stay here to raise my children.

His benevolence was well known throughout the community. Where there was need and not much money, his heart was open. Ask students who came to his office what their charges were. There was no charge. He told them they could start paying when their education was complete. Everyone—rich and poor, black and white—were children of God in Carlos' sight and were treated with equal dignity and care. As far as I was concerned, he treated both body and soul.

On a personal basis, I treasure my friend most dearly. He was a man of many talents, a *man for all seasons*. His talents and interest seemed to encompass much of the marvel of existence—gardening, bird watching, catching beauty in photographs, and bicycling through the countryside, and best of all—singing. How Carlos loved every moment, every note, every contact in Trinity's choir. We sang together some thirty years and he was ever faithful, on time, and ready to tackle any anthem the director chose. He read music well and was the cornerstone of the bass section all through the years while we sang together. How bare his chair "where late the sweet bird sang."

In our old age, Carlos and I were buddies, complete with a pact: We agreed that we would consult each other, advise each other when time came for us to quit singing, and would judge each other's failing eyes, ears, vocal chords, and faltering feet. Carlos was more honest than I. Even though he had gotten quite deaf, I couldn't tell him he wasn't hearing as he should. He knew. I asked him if my time had come and he gave a resounding, NO. Perhaps he was being kind because the time can't be too long. May I go as graciously as he.

In the *Book of Common Prayer*, we profess a belief in the communion of saints. I do so believe. When I was asked to read the lesson from Isaiah for Carlos' memorial service I said to him— *"Carlos, help me through this so I won't weep and not be able to read."* He stood there with me, and we rejoiced together at these marvelous assurances—*He will swallow up death forever, and the Lord God will wipe away tears from all faces.*

Each time a resounding deep note is sung, the organ peals out in all its glory, a flute is played, a majestic hymn is sung, Carlos is here. He is with us. From the choir invisible he sings—

Good Friends and Acquaintances

Lord, now lettest thou thy servant depart in peace
According to thy word.
For mine eyes have seen thy salvation.
Hallelujah! Hallelujah!

The Song of Simeon

17

There is a friend that sticketh closer than a brother.

Proverbs 18:24

She was the most alive personality, always looking for the ridiculous, the outlandish, the state in which you were at your worst; and, of course, she always had her camera to record whatever she found that was out-of-sight. She appeared at my house one morning, I was fresh from a weed-pulling episode, had shed my old shoes that I used in the garden and on the lawn. Flash! I was caught in my latent beauty just as I was going in the front door. There was no going back. This was Elizabeth Baddley.

Here she is —
Mrs. **Pollard Road**

Blinded by so much beauty.

Good Friends and Acquaintances

How Liz delighted in this photo. She labeled it "Mrs. Pollard Road, 1970," and showed it all over the city and the surrounding countryside, much to the delight of all who saw it. My feet were always big, "too big for my body," Mama said, and I seem to be trying to cover them up even in this unposed photo. Needless to say, this picture, much to Liz's delight, is part of our story and legends of the "nut club."

Now the original "nut club" was actually Elizabeth's creation. She rounded up all the "nutty" females she knew, put them in a special group, told them where and when to hop, and spent her days thinking up things for us to do. Her husband owned a filling station on the corner of 4th Street and Franklin, and Liz found it to be the very place for the news to accumulate and the unexplored places around the county to be discovered. She was not timid. If there were a cave to be "spelunked," we did that. If there was a restaurant we hadn't judged within a hundred miles radius, we did that even though it was at Cedar Hill. If there were a road we had never taken, we did that even though we were lost most of the day. Myriad were her ideas about having a "good time, *joie de vivre*, and look for us about sundown."

There was only one Liz Baddley. The world couldn't have had two.

Liz was a war bride. Ditching an ardent suitor to whom she was engaged, she married Tom Baddley within 6 weeks and followed him wherever Uncle Sam sent him. She was a knockout, all her beautiful, dark curly hair, her expressive eyes, her curvaceous figure, topped by the most glorious smile that said to the world, "Here am I and I'll be your friend whether you want me or not." Going with her into business offices or the office for the license for cars—anywhere—in five minutes she would have the whole place going strong with "howdy dos" and "do

Good Friends and Acquaintances

you have so and so," and on and on. She always said that there will be somebody I know or somebody who knows somebody I've heard of. She never saw a stranger. From the time she was about twenty until her death in her eighties, she had time to know two or three generations, all she loved and included. She was a people person, an admirer of all persons, old or young, fat or thin, educated or uneducated. That was Liz.

The original nut club included Maureen Batson, Jane Shelly, Evelyn Frost, Ruby Jean McCloud, and people we have long forgotten. We included through the years such personages as Mrs. Anna Belle Darden who we thought too strict for the club. We were wrong. After her first visit to the nut club, she said, "The next time you have a riot, make sure you invite me," and from then on, she was a permanent member and ready for fun.

There are two meetings that stand out in my memory. One was Liz's birthday and another, a slip-in meeting.

Now Liz was pretty careful about her birthday. She made plans for it well in advance, planning what would be the theme of the occasion and what we would do. What she didn't know was how we were going to function with a complete diversion from any birthday given in our parts. No one said a word. We didn't send cards. We didn't make any noise about how we would celebrate. We didn't do anything.

Liz lived on Eastern Hills Drive and right down the street was Margaret Telford; however, Margaret wasn't at home. We met when it was just about sunrise at Margaret's, dressed in our version of night clothes—every dilapidated or tattered gown, pajamas, hat, and curlers—with noise makers made by old pots and pans with wooden spoons. We were a motley sight. Away we marched down to Liz's with all the noise turned loose, with some of the neighbors, who weren't in on the secret, threatening to call the police.

If a sudden collapse of Eastern Hills had taken place, Liz wouldn't have been more surprised. She was in her pajamas, coffee on the stove, and getting ready to eat breakfast when we appeared on the scene. We had it all, even a birthday cake, and to top the matter off we had a bottle of "cold duck" to treat the queen for her day. The presents! The crazier, the better, and Liz got them and showed them all over town. This was a grand day, a day made just to her liking, a day to remember—wonderful, marvelous, unforgettable.

There are so many Liz stories, so many to tell that you wonder how she got them into a lifetime. There's the time Bubba Shelly dressed up as a gorilla and another time when he was a floozy dancing girl ready for anything to happen. All this took place in Liz's basement. But time has marched on and all the original "nut club" except for a very few have gone where there is a brighter day. Liz was taken from us in a most spectacular way. With some indication that something was wrong, she had two inoperable brain tumors that made her do strange things and she died from these invasions of her timeless heart.

We'll never forget her; never forget her insatiable curiosity, her love of laughter and anything on the ridiculous side. You were a person worth knowing, and she found out who you were and that right early. Never shall I cease to cherish her; she stands above all others when it came to caring. Never have I had a friend like that, and if she were here today, she would be saying, "Don't I know you? You look like Mrs. Summers out Sango way." That would be enough. From then on, she made a friend, knew who she was kin to, and how many grandchildren she had.

There was only one Liz Baddley. The world couldn't have had two. I am only glad that I had the privilege of knowing the one, the only one. God bless you, Liz, wherever you are and I know you are happy. Alleluia.

Good Friends and Acquaintances

18

All houses, wherever men have lived and died, are haunted houses.

Longfellow

At Trinity Episcopal Church a few Sundays past, Grace Lanier Brewer and I stood in the aisle and wept. She is the widow of Dr. Carlos B. Brewer, a most respected physician in Clarksville for over 40 years. We wept into a communal handkerchief, wept tears for our forsaken haunted houses, wept for our years strung together—a strand of pearls finally broken. Like the Jewish exiles in Babylon, we have hung our harps on new willows. "How shall we sing the Lord's song in a strange land when we remember Zion?" In other words, we have sold our homes.

Grace and I have different songs, different Zions; but we now share the same sense of home, the place where our marriages began, where our children were born, where we spent some 60 years of joys and sorrows whose echoes still linger in every wall, on every door knob, down every hall way. The reality is too real: We cannot go home again. Hands other than ours are the new owners of our Zions.

Grace and I are a study in a dichotomy of upbringing. She was born into a family of maids, silver spoons, chauffeurs, Episcopalism, private schooling, country clubs and Sweet Briar College. I, into a family of tobacco farming, hog killing, bean picking, schooling in a two-room school at Kirkwood, riding in a Model-T Ford and cutting my teeth on the bench back of a hellfire and damnation church. Lucky for me, my father did scrape up enough

Grace Brewer wept for Glenwood.

money for me to enroll in the Austin Peay Normal School.

This Huguenot descendant, Grace Lanier, from a family of eminent scholars, poets and statesmen, and this not too certain English-Irish-Scot of farmers and tie-hackers, have bound our disparate lives together in Clarksville. We can now sing songs of gladness and sorrow together in a beloved land.

I wept for Pollard Road.

Grace's father came from Alabama to Hopkinsville, where he owned nearby coal mines. During World War II, one of the commanding generals at Fort Campbell was Gen. Carlos B. Brewer who had a dashing son, Carlos, who met Grace Lanier in Hopkinsville.

You know the rest. After the war, they were here permanently and Carlos was my doctor, my dear friend and the chief bass note in Trinity's choir for some forty plus years. What a gem of a gentleman he was. With the ever-beautiful, ever-smiling, ever-gracious Grace making their house in Glenwood a home for their four daughters, they sang the Lord's song in a happy land.

As for me, I married a farmer-seaman who on one of his stays from the sea, bought a 360-acre cattle farm on West Fork Creek, which we promptly named "Cocklebur Haven." The cockleburs literally grew to the front door, long off its hinges and shot through by some former irate inhabitant. The discouraged porches in shame had separated themselves from the house and the roof line undulated with the passing winds. Piece by piece, we patched this mansion together and for 55 years, this was home, the place where my heart is. Last Sunday, Grace wept for Glenwood; I wept for Pollard Road.

Glenwood and Pollard Road have new owners, new makers of homes that in time, they will haunt with their memories. After we have lived these 80-plus years, Grace and I know there is no permanence, only change. With the mystery of unopened doors before us, we, by faith, trust there is another place to hang our harps, to sing our songs, to find our new Jerusalem. Our transition draws nearer and nearer.

> *For we know that if the earthly tent we live in is destroyed, we have a building from God, a house not made with hands, eternal in the heavens.*
> **II Corinthians: 5**

19

Youth is the best time to be rich, and the best time to be poor.
Euripides

How rich and poor we were in 1943. On the campus of the Austin Peay Normal School, or the Sub-Normal or the Peay Normal—whichever name displeased the administration most—this bevy of beauties held down the front lawn against the background of the Stewart Building. Gone are the great oaks, the Castle Building, the Steward Building, all having been assigned their place in history, leaving the six of us to make our ways through this past turbulent century and into another. Time has claimed three of us; time has left three.

On the other side of life are Nell Bell Cooper, Angeline Edmondson Manning, and Virginia Staton Halliburton. Left here are Christine Harris Oliver, Evelyn Randle Frost, and Charlotte Oliver Marshall. All three are eighty-six. Our family doctor, whom we know well, said that we, my husband and I, were living on "borrowed time." We joke that we take *The Leaf Chronicle* to see if our names are in the obituaries. We come; we go; that is life.

Good Friends and Acquaintances

I shall remember first my dear ones who have left us. There was that winsome Nell Bell, a charmer from Dunlop Lane, a younger sister of James William Bell. Nell joined our social whirl early on. What dances were allowed were held in homes with record-player music, and for these occasions, we, for some reason, thought we had to have a long skirt. The first time I saw Nell, she was perhaps thirteen, sporting her maxi-skirt and wearing "saddle shoes," if any one remembers saddle oxfords. She was a blond cutie, full of fun and laughter. Being two years ahead of her in high school, I didn't see too much of her until we were together again at Austin Peay State, so named as the college progressed.

Romance wise, Nell had her eye on Randall Cooper and held her breath for a date. Finally it happened. To end their first evening together, Randall stopped at Ferrell Brothers—the hamburger place across from Trinity Episcopal Church—where Nell was treated to their milk shake, noted for its quality and quantity. During this romantic interlude, Nell got quite sick at her stomach and baptized the inside of Randall's new car and washed the curb of Franklin Street. True love conquers all. Randall was a successful grocer and Nell a bridge player, par excellence. Since I never figured out a spade from a club, I did not travel in her bridge-playing circle. Their children were Linda, Charlie, and Dan.

Then there was Angeline. She was one of the rich ones. Her daddy, John Lewis Edmondson, owned a long, light blue car that Angeline was allowed to drive to school. What treasure and temptation on the back seat! Mr. Edmondson was in the tobacco business and there were samples of cigarettes and snuff on the back seat, enough to send us to you know where. How sophisticated it was to learn to smoke! Just watch old movies. Some of us gave in to temptation; some didn't. The snuff we never tried because two rivulets of juice running down both sides of our mouths would not be *de rigueur*.

Angeline was named correctly. She was an angel. She loved us all, sharing her long car, laughing a deep laugh at any sort of foolishness, and entertaining us at her family's gracious old home in the Salem community. Johnny Manning recognized these

Good Friends and Acquaintances

qualities and claimed her for his wife and mother for their four sons, all sportsmen after Johnny's own heart. Angeline, too, loved horses and field trials, making them both complement and compliment for each other. What a rich pair.

Virginia Staton Halliburton was double kin to us. She was Aunt Pud's (Frances Beaumont) daughter, Jack's first cousin. Johnny Halliburton was somehow related to me through the Rudolph Town bloodline. He is my "kissing cousin." What a loving and delightful pair they were. John Troy, Lucy, and Frances Dee are their three additions to the population. Virginia had a congenital heart problem that took her away from us too soon, leaving Johnny and all of us bereft at such a sudden loss of this multi-talented Virginia, who did all things well.

But time and loving relationships can heal many sorrows. Johnny Halliburton is the luckiest man in the world: two adoring women caring for him through his years. He suffers from Post Polio Syndrome and who blesses him now? Weena Hadley Rudolph, widow of Jack Rudolph, who always has been one who gives herself away, a true treasure. Johnny, you don't deserve all this!

Getting closer home, I come to my cousin Evelyn Randle Frost. Our mothers were sisters. Evelyn and Virginia were never tempted by Mr. Edmondson's cigarettes, but cruised with us in Angeline's long car and added much laughter to this mixture. Seems we all married hometown talent, rather a miracle with Fort Campbell nearby and with Naval Air Corp cadets on the campus. Evelyn married Jack Frost of King, Northington, and Frost, an Air Force pilot just home from the war. They had four children: Randy, Bob, Missy, and Tom. Evelyn lives now at the Regency Apartments with "Old Arthur," as she calls arthritis. She laughs through her pain and is eternally cheerful, refusing to let the crippling of her body darken the richness of her spirit.

Even closer home is Christine Harris Oliver, my sister-in-law, married to my brother, Woodson Oliver. We were from grammar school through A.P.S.U., best friends and forever "running around" together. She seemed one of the rich ones, always with a

Good Friends and Acquaintances

nickel to lend so you could buy a moon pie at Sloppy Joe Cromwell's where the raisins ran off the cookies and cigarettes were a penny a piece. Chris was the smart one, the sober one, the always totally groomed and "ironed" one, where no wrinkle dared show its face. With a memory that would shame an elephant, she knew and heard and could sing any part of four part harmony. She was the youngest of ten children, all musical. After she married my brother, they were in Atlanta for over forty years, where their son Tom was born and reared. After my brother's retirement from U.S. Steel, Hampton Station Road—the last house just before the railroad if you are driving in from Highway 79. How grand to have them here!

From left to right: Nell Bell Cooper, Angeline Edmondson Manning, Charlotte Oliver Marshall, Virginia Staton Halliburton, Christine Harris Oliver, and Evelyn Randle Frost

As for me, Charlotte Oliver Marshall, I have exposed my ignorance far and wide in *Cumberland Lore* and in my book, *Mullings and Musings*. There has been poverty and plenty in all my years from youth to this unexpected longevity. Perhaps ignorance has been nullified a bit by wisdom gleaned along four score and six years. I now know all earthly things are transient: wealth, beauty, fame, possessions, knowledge, power, and long, blue cars. But the love and relationships of this sextet of '40s pin-ups, and the fruition thereof, shall last forever. "…when the mortal puts on immortality, then shall come to pass the saying that is written: 'Death is swallowed up in victory.'"

20

The spirit of the Lord is upon me because he has anointed me to preach the gospel to the poor; to preach deliverance to the captive—to set at liberty them that are bruised.
St. Luke 4:18

The Babe of Bethlehem has come to set the captives free. What a radical claim made over 2,000 years ago, but one we have seen fulfilled in this century in our land. "Free at last, free at last!" The world has been turned upside down and the slave can rise and be benefactor, even to his former master.

When I recall the benevolence of a group of black soldiers at Fort Campbell, I know the spirit of giving and forgiving and accepting with this NCO Club's offer to donate to *Loaves & Fishes* at Christmas time. Out of a spirit of peace among men, they invited me—one of those "ugly old white women" that Fred Sanford, of TV's "Sanford and Son," held in such disdain—to be the *L&F* speaker at their December Christmas party and business meeting.

The invitation came in late November. Not having a clue where the club was, I enlisted the help of Herbert Vance, whose heart included anyone who needed help—black or white. He was the soup kitchen's main man: He brought handicapped people to lunch; kept an eye on the donation can; knew the scoop on problems with our clientele; handily assisted soup kitchen pick-ups, and when our former rector, the Rev. Bob Wood, left Trinity, Herbert made such a "thank you" speech at the going-away luncheon as to bring tears to Bob's eyes.

Until Herbert came to the rescue, I could not imagine how I could accept this invitation, even though it did mean money for *Loves and Fishes*. "Yessum, honey, I know exactly where this place is, and I will be so glad to drive you right out there because I know these people."

About the rainiest and darkest night in early December that one can imagine, I met Herbert and his veteran Oldsmobile, missing a

Good Friends and Acquaintances

taillight, at the First American Bank in New Providence. We crept out into 41-A traffic with his assurance that since he had his cataract operation he could drive without glasses and not to be too nervous, that he knew exactly where he was going. As we went down the Lafayette Road on the wrong side, I prayed an honest prayer, "Lord, if you will let me get home in one piece, I'll find a safer way to serve you."

With a long string of honking traffic behind us, we at length turned down a side road and onto a church ground whose church was graced by a neon cross ablaze in the night. Herbert announced, "See, I got you here. This is the place." The cross was not the club's lights, but then across an abandoned field he spotted more lights whose beacons led to a festive holiday celebration filled with good will, good spirits, and good food.

The Christmas party was jumping. Since Herbert had money in his pocket and was in the know with all these people, he bellied right up to the bar and said in his most authoritative voice, "Now, honey, you just get anything you want. I'm paying tonight." The lady bartender, whose fingernails would elicit a dragon's envy and her hairdo Queen Nefertiti's, eyed me with a warm condescension and included me in all the small talk around the bar. She was trying to figure out who I was—"this ugly old white woman." Perhaps she thought I was Herbert's date.

No, I didn't want beer, wine or bourbon.

When she learned from Herbert that I had come to speak and why, she gave me a pat of approval. "Now that's sweet, honey. The Lord will shine down on you." I felt a spirit there that I have missed in some "congregations of the righteous."

The party progressed, the barbecue was consumed, the pie complimented, more drinks were poured; and, as I watched the Budweiser clock over the bar come to almost 10, Mr. Chairman called the meeting to order. There were no hurried deliberations. Minutes were read and amended, the proper dress and colors and polish were discussed for participation in the upcoming Christmas

Good Friends and Acquaintances

parade, various monies were voted for present needs and charities—*Loaves & Fishes* included—questions were asked about insurance benefits and medical needs, and the hands of the clock were later and later.

At last the speaker of the evening was introduced. Mr. Chairman was brief in his introductions: "Our speaker for tonight is Mrs. ... is Mrs. ... Is Mrs. ...Well, she's from the *Loaves*." Without my qualifications being enumerated, I went into my usual *Loaves & Fishes* spiel. With all sleepy an satiated eyes on me, I kept the appeal brief because I thought it might take Herbert and me a long time to clean out the ditches on both sides of the road on our way home.

Our donation was forthcoming from the NCO Club, and I marvel at the good will of these celebrating young men. They were joyous and generous, reaching into soldier-pay pockets that might not be too flush. Most of them, no doubt had struggled to find their place in the world. Some were captives of poor schooling, racism in all its demeaning forms, perhaps malnutrition, broken family life and the cruel neighborhoods of our nation. The Army had offered them a way up, a deliverance from the bruising life that was their inheritance from slavery. The long road to freedom progresses slowly, but it does progress.

When you read the history of the anti-slavery movement in Europe and in this country, you know that the absolute foundation of this assault on captivity is the good news of the one who came to set such captives free. The inexorable and sure movement of the Holy Spirit on the hearts of many generations has delivered and is still delivering the captives across the world. The marvel of a helpless baby in a manger to span the centuries with power to topple tyrants, cruel injustices and degrading institutions is great joy indeed! "Glory to God in the highest."

Herbert and I made it back to New Providence through the rain and fog—this time continually riding the middle stripe. His parting words to me: "Now, honey, anytime you need to go anywhere at

Good Friends and Acquaintances

night, just you call me. We are helping po' people, and they ain't all black." He was proud of this night.

A loose freedom was mine as I drove home through the dark. The light of Christmas shone from my windows, and I know that this light will never go out.

P.S. Herbert Vance, my dear friend from Loves & Fishes has gone to his glory through the mysterious gate called "Death." His life here was one of love and service, and on the other side of the gate, may he go from strength to strength and into joy everlasting. I still miss him. He always called me "Honey."

GRACE ABOUNDING

21

See to it that no one fail to obtain the grace of God; that no 'root of bitterness' spring up and cause trouble.

Hebrews 12:15 RSV

"Praise Jesus, the Lord's done cleaned me up."

These words, full of laughter and joy, greeted me last Monday as I walked into *Loaves and Fishes* Soup Kitchen. Jim Thomas, the director, was away for a few days' vacation and I filled in for him, giving me once again the privilege of being with some of God's most chosen ones—maybe angels unaware.

Pat, whose Jesus testimony filled our morning, peeled carrots, chopped meat for stew, all the while filling the kitchen with her "well-springs of living water."

"Three years ago, I couldn't even smile. I was mad at ever'body, hung over from dope and alcohol, trying to get by peddling dope, and sleeping with any man for a few dollars for more dope. Couldn't nobody been a bigger mess than me. Then Jesus come along and cleaned me up, all the way up and down and sideways, and I ain't done nothing but laugh and love ever'body ever' since." As the old saying goes, I said to Pat, "I believe you've got religion*.*"

"Nome, I ain't got religion. Religion's no good cause so many folks say they got it, but they ain't got Jesus. He can take all that nasty meanness out of you, but sometime religion just make you meaner. You gotta have Jesus. His love is free and he sets you free and makes you laugh all over."

Pat's joyous testimony rattled my small grasp of grace and found me looking at my meanness and unresolved anger. Jesus hasn't been too successful with cleaning me up, and I fear I have "roots of bitterness" springing up that will make briar patches or thorn trees unless I root them out. Barbara Brown Taylor, rector of Grace-Calvary Church in Clarkesville, Ga., calls this bitterness "Arthritis of the Spirit."

Barbara Brown Taylor writes: "If God is willing to stay with me in spite of my meanness, my weakness, my stubborn self-righteousness, then who am I to hold those same things against someone else?" Better I should confess my own sins than keep track of yours, only it is hard to stay focused on my shortcomings. I would so much rather stay focused on yours, especially when they are hurtful to me.

Staying angry with you is how I protect myself from you. Refusing to forgive you is not only how I punish you; it is also how I keep you from getting close enough to hurt me again, and nine times out of ten it works, only there is a serious side effect. It is called bitterness, and it can do terrible things to the human body and soul. I can usually learn something from my anger, and if I am lucky I can use the energy of it to push for change in myself or in my relationships with others. Often I can see my own part in what I am angry about, and that helps, because if I had a hand in it then I can concentrate on getting my hand back out of it again instead of spinning my wheels in blame. I can, in other words, figure out what my anger has to teach me and then let it go, but when my anger goes on and on without my learning or changing anything then it is not plain anger anymore. It has become bitterness instead. It has become resentment, which is "arthritis of the spirit."

To forgive is to give up the exhilaration of one's own unassailable rightness. And there is loss in that, only it is the loss of an illusion, and what is gained is unmistakably real: the chance to live again, free from the bitterness that draws the sweetness from our lives, that gives us scary faces and turns us into carrion crows who blot out the sun with our flapping. No one else does this to us. We do it to ourselves, but we do not have to.

Pat, my new Soup Kitchen friend, knew this chance to live again, free from the bitterness and anger that took the sweetness out of her life.

"You know, Miss Charlotte, Jesus so good to us, and he wants me to thank all yo'all." She handed me a packages of chocolate-chip cookies tied with a yellow ribbon, holding this message, "Thank you for serving Jesus."

These words of St. Paul came to me: "When I came to you, brethren, I did not come proclaiming to you the testimony of God in lofty words or wisdom. For I decided to know nothing among you except Jesus Christ and him crucified." 1 Cor. 2

22

Let all bitterness, and wrath, and anger, and clamor, and evil speaking be put away from you, with all malice: And be ye kind one to another, tenderhearted, forgiving one another, even as God for Christ's sake has forgiven you.

Ephesians 4:31-32

Have you seen the bumper sticker that reads—"Have you hugged someone today?" Having been reared in a family of not too much physical touching, hugging, and kissing, I have found it awkward at times to be too "touchy-feely", fearing to be a dirty old woman. Never too late to learn! Of late, I have had some tenderhearted-teaching, some valuable lessons in the warmth of loving touch with no implications other than Christ's tender mercies.

In December, I worked with Trinity's team at *Loaves and Fishes* on our appointed day, the third Wednesday of the month. Christmas Day was near. A round little woman with slightly crossed eyes and a measure of retardation written on her face came by the serving table to thank us for her meal. With imploring eyes, she looked at me and asked, "Can I hug you?" With that, we fell into each others' arms with a tremendous hug and a re-hug and a kiss-on-the-cheek, and I said to her, "I hope Santa Claus is good to you." Her reply was with a vacant sadness. "Santa Claus never comes to see me, and my meals and my friends at this kitchen are my Christmas." She had no other, she declared. Probably forgotten by her family, she in her loneliness needed the feel of someone she judged to care, and I had the privilege to be that one. Mickey's sermon of being the Body of Christ, the ones left here to be his loving presence, came alive in me.

January brought another of Christ's own to our kitchen. Near closing time, a new face appeared—a lovely, slender black girl, well-groomed and well-mannered, who announced in no uncertain voice—"I am so hungry." The bounty of this ministry is a miracle that makes you understand the miracle of Christ's feeding the five thousand. She had two trays and ate the last crumb. When she was leaving and we were winding up serving at 12:00, she turned around at the door and came back with the same request to this old white woman. "I need a hug real bad." There were tears in our eyes and she looked at me after a long embrace and blessed me, "May God bless you every day." She left, back into her world that only she and God know. My prayer for this slip-of-a-girl is that she can come to know that nothing can separate her from the love of God and that she is made worthy by this love.

At Trinity, we have gotten good at hugs, at least in the choir. At first we were a bit hesitant to carry-on so, away from our laced-up ways. Actually, the Peace came from the Jewish liturgy, and if you read their prayer book—we have a copy in our library—you will find how much our prayer book owes to this Jewish foundation. Remember all the first Christians were Jews.

Going back to hugs, there are some fine huggers here at Trinity and they hug away from the Peace. One I never dreamed would be my hugger. He is a military man who puts up at times an opinionated and argumentative front, but who, on the inside, is a softy, a soul who is forever seeking, questioning, and learning, and with a true measure of poetry in his inner-most being. What a tender-hearted friend.

The other I shall name: One Richard Gildrie who just this Sunday past gave me a bear hug that has lasted all the week. How I treasure this good man's acceptance of me as a huggable traveler and for his wise humility, a star to follow. He helps me comprehend the incomprehensible—the writings from the first Epistle of John.

"Beloved let us love one another; for love is of God, and he who loves is born of God and knows God. He who does not love does not know God for GOD IS LOVE" Wow!!

23

Unto us a child is born, unto us a son is given.
Isaiah 9:6

As the birthday of two Christmas babies approaches, I mull and muse the miracle of birth with its promises. One of these births recorded is of the flesh—the other of the spirit. Fitting into the retelling of these old stories are two Marys: Mary a country girl of this country and Mary a peasant girl of Palestine. Even though separated by two thousand years, these maidens could have compared notes about their early engagements, the supportive men they had for husbands and the birth of their firstborn sons while they were teenagers. "Who would believe their report?"

Mary Beaumont Marshall was God's original. Growing up in a St. Bethlehem community of staid ideas of lady-like deportment and suitable education, she cared not a fig. "Mammy," as Mary called her mother, decreed that her daughters would have every opportunity of the education available at this time, perhaps teach school a year or two, and find themselves husbands from the local gentry, ones well-established with promising prospects.

At fifteen, Mary Beaumont was a rebel with a cause. Jim Marshall had ridden by her school on his horse. Instantly, he was her man! Her older sister, Frances Beaumont Staton, was the teacher at their one-room school, Willoughby Shack; and any assignment Frances gave Mary, Mary would reply, "If you want these problems done, do them yourself." She had another pursuit in mind, this pursuit being only Jim. With her academic record in limbo, Mary was sent home to "help Mammy."

This irrepressible soul could not be thwarted. When she was seventeen, she nailed Jim down for matrimony, sending him home to his long-widowed mother with their plans. Jim's mother ask him—"Jim, where shall you live?" and his reply—"Here with you and Uncle Jack Fry." What a beginning of a long, lovely story.

Mary Beaumont Marshall was God's original. The couple pictured on their 50th wedding anniversary.

They were married in February 1921, spent a night with Uncle Alf Killebrew for their honeymoon, and Mary gave birth on December 28, 1921, to my husband, Jack Fry Marshall, a most-welcomed Christmas present. He weighed in at ten pounds and Dr. John Ross, (Dorothy Ann Russo's father) looking at this young mother, told her she should still be playing with dolls.

This son of Mary's great passion for Jim has "risen up to call her blessed" and has become, as the oldest son, a patriarch in his time.

Grace Abounding

He could not "give his life as a ransom for many," but many through the years have known that his life has been for them. The first "Bishop of Rossview", Mary Beaumont Marshall, was well-pleased with her first-born son and she hid nothing in her heart.

Across two thousand years, I ponder another Mary who was probably about my mother-in-law's age. As was the custom in those days, her family had betrothed her to Joseph, a good and just man, and she had no chasing to do. Liking romantic illusions, I trust that her eyes were for him only and that she longed to be the mother of his children.

Luke's story is the mystical one. Being Greek and writing to the Gentile world, he was familiar with the stories of gods descending to mankind and angels being the messengers of God. Gabriel was busy. He had Elizabeth, Zachariah, Mary, and Joseph to convince and inspire. But, what of poor little Mary? What will the neighbors say? What will Joseph do?

What of Mary's schooling? Like Mary Beaumont, she may have avoided scholarly pursuits. As was the custom in those days, only the males were educated. However, she knew Jewish poetry because her brilliant *Magnificat* was based on the Prayer of Hannah (1 Samuel 2:1-10); or Luke, the author, could have interspersed this song of Mary into the Christmas story for artistic appeal, a device often used in Scriptures. He included also the Song of Zachariah and Simeon, no doubt with the *Book of Common Prayer* in mind!!

"Mary kept all these things, pondering them in her heart." Oh, to know of Mary's ponderings. If Mary knew she had borne Jesus, the Messiah, why was she disturbed when she found him in the temple, in his Father's house? Once Jesus seemed to have put his whole family down. "My mother and my brothers are those who hear the word of God and do it." Did she know the prophets and that the Messiah would suffer and be crucified? As recorded in John's gospel, she stood at the cross. Did she know the gift she had given the world? The Catholic world has all these questions answered, while fools rush in to mull and muse.

Great debts we owe to our Marys. The gifts of life and love and example, and ultimately, our salvation are from Mary of Palestine. Unto us sons and daughters are given. May the Prince of Peace reign in our hearts until He comes to reign forever and ever. Alleluia!

24

Over and over I have mused at Jesus' words in the 18th chapter of Matthew's gospel. They have haunted me as he defines greatness and tells of the angels who care for little children.

"See that you do not despise one of these little ones; for I tell you that in heaven their angels always behold the face of my father who is in heaven…So it is not the will of my father that one of these little ones should perish."

In my new understanding, these words of our Lord say to me that each innocent child has his own angel who knows him, who loves him, who protects him, and in the final consummation will turn all children's pain into joys untold.

The pain is in their eyes. On my street, one mother puts her children outside, rain or shine, and they must be forbidden to come in until a certain hour. As I pass by, they sit forlorn, huddled on their doorstep, or sometime wander toward the street. One day I stopped for a little girl—three or four years old—to tell her to be careful of the cars. With great fear-filled eyes she ran from me; perhaps her mother had told her to never talk to strangers. What awaited her inside her home? What is her angel saying to the Father as the child beholds His face?

Going far from my street to Darfur in the Sudan, my heart is pierced by the starving babies, clinging with tree-frog hands to their mother's dry breasts as she entreats for some assistance that cannot be found. Their eyes mirror the hunger of the ages. My over-sated stomach is sickened. "Father, where are their angels? Must they wait until heaven? If so, their dying will be joy and you will take them into your arms."

Little girls are not allowed on the streets of Iraq, but little boys seem to abound. As they stand by bombed-out cars—we are never allowed to see the actual carnage and gore on our televisions—their eyes reflect a culture as old as the Garden of Eden, and these children behold the sight of Abel's blood crying from the ground. It cries louder and louder and the deep anguish is in all eyes who know the failure to love.

If we love little children and are told as Christians not to despise any of these little ones, what have we wrought upon these innocents? If we loved our neighbors as ourselves, we would be in sack cloth and ashes, forgetting other nation's failures and looking into our own. Who will condemn us and turn God's face from our sins? Where are our prophets? Where are our William Sloan Coffins, our Bonhoeffers? Are they muted by a national self-righteous theocracy which declares criticism unpatriotic? Our silence is deafening, and the angel of each abandoned child will have us look into the face of God. Who among us can stand?

May God's all embracing grace and forgiveness have mercy on us all.

25

And he shall turn the hearts of the fathers to the children, and the hearts of the children to their fathers

Malachi 4

And a little child shall lead them.

Isaiah 11:6

In Atlanta, a young Joseph knew the time was close when his Mary's days would be accomplished and she would be delivered. They weren't married, and she had already been put away by her first husband who had left her with three small children. Joseph's devout family, his church, and the gossipmongers declared this Joseph and Mary to be disowned, banished from communion, a general disgrace to Buckhead society.

Joseph's parents had two older children, safely married in just the right church and circle, but by reason of thumbing their noses at the Pope or through some problem that the medical world could not correct, they had never produced any grandchildren. These parents were bereft, having saved their carefully and correctly churched love for this longed-for new generation. Ten barren years went by. Joseph, the younger son by several years, went off into a far country. Country clubs, the right families with the right daughters and the right dogmas preached by his family and church sent him away to this new place to find himself.

In a little town on the sea coast of Georgia, this younger son came to himself as a grease monkey, a fixer of all sorts and conditions of motors and machines. To add to his fixing, he found a restorer for his heart. His Mary, with her three children, filled a void that he had never before recognized, a void cold and empty, left to him by years of deprivation of a love that would not let him go.

Mary's divorce was not final, so Joseph, because of his upbringing, could not consider marriage, yet there was this pregnancy. He would not put Mary away, for she was great with child; therefore, unto them a child was born—a beautiful son was given. Joseph pondered all these things in his heart and set about being father to four small children, all without any blessing in the temple.

And it came to pass that these tidings of great joy got back to Atlanta: "Unto us a grandchild is born." The grandparents said one to another, "Let us now go even unto the sea shore and see this thing which is come to pass, which the Lord has made known to us." And they came with haste and found Mary and Joseph, and the baby lying, not in a manger, but in their son's arms. A little child had led them to follow the star and to bring gifts of gold and reconciling love to the babe's cradle by the sea.

This is a true story. The names have been changed to protect the innocent. The advent of a grandchild so melted the hearts of this careful couple that they became grandparents to Mary's other children, showering on them all the stored-up love that finally broke the dam of their outworn dogmas and shallow values. Their hearts were forever turned to these children, and in return, the children's hearts were forever turned to their "Granny and Poppa."

Rules were relaxed; there was a grand wedding with much rejoicing and at the last report, college scholarships had been set up for Mary and Joseph's children. Joseph's mother so turned her heart to her daughter-in-law that she made a wish for more grandchildren. Mary kept all these things and pondered them, knowing her child had brought about a miracle of heart turning.

This love that changes all is ours for the taking. We can forgive, we can accept, we can turn our old selves upside down, we can start anew after any mistake, we can love without reservation, for that is the love the child brought us two thousand years ago. Let us rejoice!

"And suddenly there was with the angels a multitude of the heavenly host praising God and saying, 'Glory to God in the highest, and on earth peace, good will toward men.'"

May the little child lead us and keep us in the New Year and through all our years.

HELLFIRE

26

You blind guides, who strain out a gnat and swallow a camel.

Matthew 23

Dull and dreary, winter is with us again. Traditionally this has been our light-hearted time with "jest and jollity" to brighten these short days. Having revealed many family foibles and personal exposures, I found scant scrapings at the bottom of the funny barrel when there was a sudden upsurging. Cousin Bessie had taken her gnat-straining to her most restrictive heaven, that place where only ones of her denomination and baptism could possibly go. She declared all issues either "scriptural" or "non-scriptural" depending on what the Bible said or what it didn't say. Eternal damnation and hellfire were her specialties.

Having been consigned there by Bessie's theology, dare I write of this hot subject while she watches me from the parapets of Glory? Not being too scriptural, I'll take a chance. Cousin Bessie, better known behind her back as Cousin Asbestos, knew the dimensions—depth, height, breadth and square miles—of Hell, its temperature, the ones already roasting there and the ones here who had not followed her scriptural guidance and would be Hell's predestined denizens. Her poor husband, Cousin Charlie, had already gone to his assigned front seat in the inferno where she declared he would need an asbestos suit. Therefore the name—Cousin Asbestos.

"Now, Charlie, Hell is not half full." Sunday after Sunday, she harangued him to come to her church—the only one which preached real salvation and true scriptural baptism. All other mealy-mouthed, whitewashed preaching was an open door to hell, and you must be baptized on the spot of your profession of faith lest you die between your saving and your submerging. Bessie always trotted out Phillip and the eunuch because Phillip's baptism was down in the water—both Phillip and the eunuch, absolutely scriptural. There was none of that Methodist "dry-cleaning."

Cousin Charlie knew how the world wagged. He had experienced so much hell in the here-and-now with Cousin Bessie that this hot place sounded like a spot where he and his buddies might hang out. Dancing, card-playing and a nip here and there were his passions, and why Cousin Bessie took him on as salvageable no one could ever guess. She said it was scriptural to try and save the lost, and she was giving her life to warning sinners about the fiery pit where the flames burn forever and the worms never die.

One Christmas Eve at the family party, Cousin Charlie had a few good celebrations and proceeded to roll himself up in a scatter rug in front of the fireplace and announced in a loud voice as he was rolling, "I done told Bessie to bury me in a fur coat in case Hell freezes over. You've got to go prepared." Cousin Bessie, whose mouth stayed in a perpetual crimp, opened it long enough to be unscriptural with expletives tuned to G and D sharp, blasphemy appropriate for Charlie's pool room. The camel was swallowed.

With true Christmas spirits and tidings of great joy, we retreated to the front hall and celebrated Cousin Charlie's liberating the Christmas party. What wonder there is in laughter. How tedious it is to be scriptural. Cousin Bessie unrolled Charlie and took him home, leaving us, the unscriptural, well into the night. We drank a few gnats and smoked a few camels.

The liberating event of all time has come to us in the form of an innocent baby in a manger. He has come to give us life abundant and to free us from straining picky little gnats and swallowing big hairy camels. His Christmas gift to all is the love that forgets the scriptural and leads us into the spiritual, into that place of acceptance of ourselves and our neighbors.

For the New Year let us give up being blind guides, knowing how our neighbors should conduct themselves. Let us give up our hang-ups on every gnat hair of proper performing of liturgy, the absolute correct vestments, and whether to kneel or stand. The Christ child is looking on our hearts. Let us concentrate on the weightier matters of the Law—kindness, acceptance of all in our human condition, mercy for those under great burdens, forgiveness, and let us hear anew Christ's command: "A new commandment I give you that you love one another." This is the law that banished all gnats and camels. We are free to be who we are—God's children and joint heirs with our older brother, the Christ Child.

When Cousin Bessie vowed that she did everything that the Bible said do, I asked her, "Do you greet all the brethren with a holy kiss?" She hasn't answered me yet. So I greet you all with a holy kiss for 2008. "God bless us, every one."

27

Now there was a day when the sons of God came to present themselves before the Lord, and Satan came among them. The Lord said to Satan, "Whence have you come?" Satan answered the Lord, "From going to and fro on the earth, and walking up and down on it."

Job 1:6 and 7

We three children—my brother and sister and I—would lie on the floor on our stomachs, feet in the air, and study this picture of the "Devil Fishing" until we completely smudged the page of this ragged old book of hellfire and damnation, left to our father by one of his grandfathers. This "Old Devil" was real!

After a red hot sermon from St. Peter telling us that Satan was prowling around like a roaring lion looking for someone to devour, we knew that he was not only walking to and fro but that he would "eat us up" if we didn't behave. Old aunts would remind us—"The Bad Man is going to get you." On our Sunday school cards, God was always up on a cloud, book in hand, no doubt keeping score. Evilly leering around a tree trunk was the Devil, pitch fork in hand, ready to barbecue us over his eternal fire. Thus God and the Devil were anthropomorphized—a fancy word ascribing human form to non-human entities. As we progressed to the upper Sunday school classes, we were schooled and re-schooled about a perfect man, Job, totally innocent before God; but God let Satan completely destroy Job, except for his life. Here began the eternal question of why the innocent suffer. God and the Devil had a bet that Job would curse God and die. We knew the ending so we always bet on Job.

The story of Job is an ancient folk tale, circulated orally, back to the second millennium BC. It was written down in Hebrew during the time of David and Solomon and rewritten by an anonymous poet of the Exile, sixth century BC. In my time, I have seen the Book of Job in dramatic form with God, Job, Job's wife, and his comforters on stage. Some of the most glorious poetry of the ages is God's reply to Job out of a whirlwind. Read it.

We would lie on the floor on our stomachs, feet in the air, and study this picture of the "Devil Fishing."

Though I doubt there was ever a totally innocent man and a God so heartless as to turn all evil loose on a mere mortal, I will ask the literalist among us to forgive my questions. Innocence still suffers and Satan yet walks around and devours you and me with his subtle, just-right-for-us, temptations. How many times he has fished me out of his pond. If I were Roman Catholic, I would have worn out the hinges on the door for the confessors, forever elaborating on the truth, not loving my neighbor, and still admiring good looking men, with mostly rust—not lust. Scripture reminds us that the tongue is the most uncontrolled of all our members. There's Satan with lightning out of our mouths. How we gossip, slander, judge, criticize, curse, and sometime bless from this one aperture. We are the ones Satan has empowered to devour.

Hellfire

My mama knew well the Old Devil's walking around. He walked over two of her uncles, making her a teetotaler and a member of the *Women's Christian Temperance Union* for her life. One uncle, who was a widower, took the bottle bait, leaving his four children alone for days and was found lying in a roadside ditch, dead, from too much alcohol and too much snow. Another uncle took the heart bait. As Satan reeled in another big fish, Mama's uncle died as he got on the train at Hackberry with an irate husband's bullet in his belly. Innocence always suffers. The uncle left a wife and a four year old daughter.

Satan didn't know about drugs when he had his picture drawn for this book. This scourge in our lifetime has become the most dangerous bait for the present generation. Personally, in our family, I have seen this temptation destroy the most talented of all the grandsons. Last week at our grocery store, I saw the drug world at its worst. A lovely grandmother, well in her sixties, was left to rear two beautiful boys, ages six and two. Her daughter and her husband—she didn't know where, addicted to whatever—left the grandmother and grandfather the responsibilities of their children's welfare.

Satan's temptations know no bounds, and one of the big ones is bound to be money. The almighty dollar catches big fish. The Devil dangles the bait and from our economic news of late, he has reeled in some trophies that have been stuffed and are installed behind prison walls. Cheating, stealing, and lying go hand in hand with this bait and at times seem the standard of Wall Street, leaving many innocent to suffer.

Some may not see card playing as a bait. They haven't tried poker for money. At our country church, regular playing cards were called "spot cards," and we were limited to Rook and Old Maid. Cousin Bob, bless him yet, ruined his family's business by his obsessive gambling, and as a final result, took his own life rather than face the shame of squandering his family's security.

Satan knows that our pride is the one thing that gets us all. We use every means to prop up our small selves to make us feel real on the inside. That's where all our false gods get in the bait bucket: possessions, more possessions, big cars, big houses, big diamonds, big ideas, big appetites that fatten our emptiness to the ruination of our bodies. Satan, you've got me. My stomach is too big, along with my mouth. Small is my empathy to this neighbor I am supposed to love as I love myself. With St. Paul I ask, "Who will deliver me from this body of death?" Who will rescue me from drowning in Satan's fish pond? Who indeed?

It will have to be the good fisher-of-men. We need another picture in our ragged book of this fisherman who sees us afar off, comes running to the rim of the pond, grabs us up out of the mud and mire, cleans us up, puts on us new clothes, and then celebrates with our getting out of our big messes with a great fish fry. What a joyous relief.

Satan, you just walk on by and take your stinking bait with you. We will stay here where we are loved and forgiven and accepted no matter what you did to us. We shall try to learn from this fisherman who loves absolutely, unconditionally. His wonder has been shown to us. Get your buckets ready for some real fishing and let us hear the Good Fisherman's call—"Follow Me."

HISTORY

28

*I must go down to the sea again, to the lonely sea and the sky.
And all I ask is a tall ship and a star to steer her by.*

"Sea Fever"—John Masefield

Our state, being totally landlocked, does not call its inhabitants down to the sea in ships. The call can only come from the hearing of the ear and the imagining of the mind as a wild wind whips through a shrouded cornfield or an icy rain lashes the windowpanes at night.

To Rossview in 1929 came a retired sea captain from Texas, one who had abandoned the sea in favor of matrimony, his bride being the most reluctant one who ever marched down the aisle, and who always refused to bear her husband's name. She was Rossview's first liberated woman, one of an exquisite and inquiring mind and one who had traveled to foreign climes where she met Captain V.O. Park. On her mailbox was boldly stated: "Mary Hallums" and underneath "V.O. Park." These two were to be an influence on a young life that would send one of Rossview's sons away "to a tall ship and a star to steer her by."

Across Dunlop Lane from Miss Mary and Mr. Owen lived a farm boy who hung on Captain Park's stories of the sea and exotic ports-of-call and who delved into their library of *National Geographic*, myriad periodicals, and books from antiquity to the present time. "Miss Mary and Mr. Owen," we said, "had a literary turn," and, in turn, you could hardly find a place to sit because each inch was packed and stacked into some library semblance with newspapers cascading from ceiling-high piles along the walls. No printed matter was ever thrown out. Miss Mary insisted that someone would need these references. Thus, through his boyhood, this lad sat enthralled by the old captain's sea stories and found in their reading rooms a time and tide away from his landlocked home.

During World War II because of the critical need for farm products, farm boys could be exempt from the draft, but one callow youth on Dunlop Lane said, "I must go down to the sea in ships," and away he launched himself to St. Petersburg, Fla., where he enlisted in the Merchant Fleet, as ordinary seaman. Captain Park's talks had done their work. This lad was to be my husband, Jack Fry Marshall.

Four war years he sailed many hazardous voyages, being spared the Murmansk run only by kind fortune. The Merchant Fleet had the highest casualty rate of any branch of the services and was denied veterans' status because the men had to sign on the ships through the old organized unions. Now these men have full veterans' status. Among them were men of the highest order: my husband's best friend, a lawyer; ones who had failed their physicals; those too old for enlistment; patricians from "up east" who purely loved sailing those vessels; and those with "sea fever."

Jack enlisted in the Merchant Marine Fleet as ordinary seaman.

Jack's ships were usually T-2 tankers, which carried high-octane gasoline across the North Atlantic to the Allied force based in England. The German U-boats were in their most lethal wolf packs—one strike from their submarines and you were gone—no survivors from the flaming sea.

For some time after the war, my husband continued to go to sea so we could buy his dreamed-of farm. In the meantime, he had worked his way up the ship's ladder from ordinary seamen to ship's captain and had been awarded this service's highest medal for heroism, having risked his life in a typhoon in the Indian Ocean to save the lives of the crew of a French destroyer.

Mr. Owen's sea tales were calm compared to Jack's and when Jack came home he always had long visits with Mr. Park, who in his old age had become quite nostalgic about the sea, longing for one more voyage before he furled his sails.

After the war, Jack made arrangements with his company and signed Mr. Park on as second mate on the S.S. Producer, and away those two old salts sailed from Houston to Korea and back to the West Coast. Mr. Owen declared to all that Jack was the best captain in his experience. He had never known a ship to run so smoothly. Little did he know that the captain had warned all the crew that there was a special person aboard, one almost like a father.

After the war, Jack made arrangements with his company and signed Mr. Park on as second mate on the S.S. Producer.

Children are such priceless repositories of potential. You never know what some kindness or shared stories, or a library, or a word of encouragement can bring forth. How precious a gift was this loving friendship of two older people to a boy who knew little beyond his bucolic world. They gave him a new star to steer by. Their kindness came round to more kindness by a younger seaman to an older seaman. "What goes around comes around."

When you go to the cemetery at Grace Chapel, find the headstones of Mary Hallums and V.O. Park. Miss Mary's epitaph is thus inscribed: "Be not the first by whom the new is tried, nor yet the last to lay the old aside."—Alexander Pope. Underneath is carved the "Lamp of Learning."

Mr. Owen's epitaph is this: "The use of traveling is to regulate imagination by reality; and instead of thinking how things may be, to see them as they are."—Samuel Johnson. For him, the "Mariner's Wheel."

When Jack and I are at rest at Grace Chapel, may we, too, leave behind some young persons who have known our interest and our love. Could this be a fitting epitaph for us?

> *My bounty is as boundless as the sea, my love as deep; and more I give to thee, the more I have, for both are infinite.*
>
> **Shakespeare from Romeo and Juliet**

History

29

Author's note: This Mullings and Musings was written for the October 2001 issue of our church paper. September 11 had just happened to our shocked nation. Looking back and rereading this front page, I decided to publish it again and let us ponder anew these thoughts that came to me at this time in our nation's history. Abraham's sons—Isaac and Ishmael—have made no progress in reconciliation, and will we as the world's greatest power depend on "shock and awe" and live with the shame of raw military power? Where is our allegiance to the Prince of Peace?

> Let us build a city and a tower, whose top may reach unto heaven and let us make us a name.
>
> ***Genesis***

Our Tower of Babel has come down and our tongues are confused. Who can pronounce judgment on such evil? Who can send forth words of comfort and mercy? Who can declare wisdom and understanding? Who can forewarn of further evil among us; and finally, who can give utterance to words of forgiveness and reconciliation in the face of our need for revenge? What mighty hand has brought down our towers?

Height has forever equated power. God speaks to us from "on high". Moses had to go twice to the heights of Mt. Sinai where the Law was burned into his very countenance. The Pharaohs, presenting themselves as gods, built the great pyramids that are here today but will, in centuries to come, crumble to dust. The Colossus of Rhodes, one of the seven wonders of the ancient world, came down in an earthquake before the time of Christ, as did the great lighthouse at Pharos in the 1300s. The cathedrals of Europe, built to express the glorious transcendence of God, will like all manmade edifices be shaken from their foundations. Is there no permanence in man's great towers?

History

From Moses on Mt. Sinai, there is permanence—the Law—the foundation that was laid that judges all towers in all ages: "The first is 'Hear, O Israel: The Lord our God is one; and you shall love the Lord your God with all your heart, and with all your soul, and with all your mind and with all your strength.' The second is this: 'You shall love your neighbor as yourself.' Then, as St. Paul reminds us, 'Love does not wrong to a neighbor; therefore, love is the fulfilling of the Law.'"

We ask in our distress, "Why are we so cast down? Why are we hated by millions around the world? What great evil is ours? Why have our towers come down upon us?" From the towering heights of Mt. Sinai comes the Mighty Word that we have disobeyed. We cannot love our neighbor and God rightly. We have been weighed in the balance and found wanting. "There is none good, no, not one."

Before Moses and the Law, Abraham and Sarah heard God's promise of a great nation through a son and obeyed him, but coldly forgot his love for all his creation. Hagar, the slave girl, and Ishmael, her illegitimate son by Abraham, were cast out into the desert to die. God heard the weeping of Hagar and Ishmael "and the angel of God called to Hagar and said to her, 'What troubles you, Hagar? Fear not, for God has heard the voice of the lad where he is. Arise, lift up the lad and hold him fast with your hand; for I will make him a great nation.'" Each year when the Nations of Islam make their pilgrimage to Mecca, they retrace the ordeal of Hagar in the wilderness. Both Isaac's and Ishmael's descendants see themselves as the true heirs of Abraham, the beloved of God, the children of promise.

To read the story of the three great religions of the world and to try to comprehend their hatred and slaughter through the centuries is to recoil in horror. Holy wars have taken more blood than all other conflicts. We Christians are guilty of the crusades, the inquisition, the religious wars that decimated Europe, the destruction of the Native Americans, and the hanging of witches at Salem. Where was our love? We dehumanize our neighbors, making them into vermin to be destroyed, forgetting that God so loved the world,

History

which includes all Arabs and their leaders. Can we never overcome Evil with Good?

Israel has been re-established after its long exile, the Diaspora. This is the fulfillment of their interpretation of Jewish prophecy. After the Holocaust, the Jews were determined to return to the Promised Land, their inheritance from Abraham. With their unequivocal claim to Jerusalem, they displaced the Palestinians, took their homes and land, and many of these heirs of Ishmael have lived three generations in refugee camps that are hotbeds of hatred and revenge.

From the World Trade Towers in New York City, billions of dollars have flowed across the Atlantic to establish an oasis of luxury in the midst of homelessness and poverty. Our country has been the source of much of this wealth, and the Pentagon has armed Israel with all its latest weaponry, both on land and in the air. The Palestinians have rocks, some smaller arms and the final desperate act—terrorism.

The Israelis have not loved their neighbors as themselves, and we in our country are guilty of pride and the arrogance of power, the cardinal sin of mankind. If we do rebuild the towers, "let us sit down first and count the cost."

In our beloved country's defense, we are full of pride but are filled with pity; we wound but we have no peer in binding up wounds; we condemn and then comfort; we are a paradox of every nation, come together in this new land to grope for a new way of living and loving. We have much to learn. Would that we had a Marshall Plan for the distressed peoples in the Middle East, a plan that would call us to be servants, to give ourselves away in reconciliation. We should set our hearts on that. "Vengeance is mine," says the Lord, and let us not live and die by the sword, but live from the everlasting heights of the Law of Love. Christ came to show us the way.

History

30

Onward Christian soldiers marching as to war with the cross of Jesus going on before. Christ the royal master leads against the foe; forward into battle see his banner go.

The Hymnal

In some Christian circles this old hymn has been shunned as too militaristic. Their Jesus, the Prince of Peace, would never have his people marching as to war, his banner never leading against any foe who might become his disciple. "Blessed are the peace makers for they shall be called the children of God" and "Blessed are the meek for they shall inherit the earth." There's no marching into battle, no triumph songs, no shouts of victory—but hungering and thirsting after righteousness, their pure hearts following their Master's example.

Through the centuries, "Crowns and thrones may perish, kingdoms rise and wane." They all have—I know of no exception. There have been enough "Holy Wars" to overflow Heaven and Hell, and the tragedy of all tragedies is that we never learn. "I won't forgive you or understand you; instead, I will kill you. We'll live by the sword and die by the sword. Shame on those sissy peacemakers."

Thus I mull and muse with some wild-eyed, radical, idealistic "what-ifs" and some "it-might-have-beens." What Christian among us ever "joined this happy throng and blended your voices in the triumph song?" What if we tried it! Tried it just once?

What if after 9/11, we as Christians decided to forgive this dreadful act? Three thousand of our citizens perished! We must strike back with our powerful sword and put these terrorist under a barrage that shall eradicate them from the face of the earth. But "what-if"? What if the millions of Christians in our country said "NO"; we shall follow our Christ. Instead of the billions spent on daisy-cutter bombs, smart bombs, stealth bombers, Black Hawks, and armored vehicles and ammunition, we shall take those billions and love our neighbors. We shall launch a mighty armada of ships and we as Christ-in-the-world shall go to our enemies and invade them with forgiving love, expressed in food, housing, education, and ultimately freedom. Dictators cannot stand with the overcoming of evil with good.

What if the gallant soldiers and marines of our nation were sent in with the same intent? No great bombing raids, no swift fleet of horrors to kill Iraqi sons, with each mother having these dragon's teeth sowed in her heart. With the same mother-love in our country, "what-if" there were no messengers of death to come to the door?

In the year 2005, can we as a nation make some of the might-have-beens into reality? With our supposedly Christian majority, how can we answer to our Lord when he asks us if we were blessed peacemakers, did we love our enemies, who are our neighbors, and did we beat our swords into plow shares? As our billions flow into Mars' terrible maw, "what-if" we are answered by His terrible swift sword? "His truth is marching on."

31

He (Elisha) went up from there to Bethel; and while he was going up on the way, some small children came out of the city and jeered at him saying, 'Go up, you baldhead! Go up, you baldhead!' and he turned around and when he saw them, he cursed them in the name of the Lord. And two she-bears came out of the woods and tore forty-two of the children.

2 Kings 2:23-25

If I had been the Jewish historian writing Second Kings, I would have left this story out. Shame on Elisha; shame on the Lord for listening to this curse. Elisha had just requested from Elijah—"I pray you let me inherit a double share of your spirit," and he had seen Elijah taken up alive in a chariot of fire into Heaven, and the mantle of the greatest of prophets had fallen on him—and this is the way he responded to a group of teasing children! Perhaps they didn't believe the story of Elijah's "going up" and wanted to see this baldhead go up. I don't know, but it certainly seemed shabby to curse the children and call on the Lord to send two she-bears to tear them apart. The writers, too, got a jab at the females. Where were the he-bears?—waiting, like the male lions, for the females to do all the work and then banish them from the feast? These Old Testament writers shifted the blame rather like Flip Wilson: "The Devil made me do it." The Lord was the whipping boy for all this mayhem, brought on by a vain prophet.

However, in Elisha's defense, there is something about hair. Everyone knows about bad hair days. If your hair's not right, you feel edgy all over. Therefore, we tousle, tease, color, perm, straighten, cut and curl; and if we are male, we Rogaine, comb-over, dye, implant, and as a final desperate act—toupee. Too bad Elisha didn't have a good stylist so the hairs of his head wouldn't be numbered.

Throughout these Jewish scholars' history of their conquests, the Lord supposedly told these chosen people to kill all in the invaded lands—even the cattle—flatten their cities and leave only a burning heap. What had happened to God's commandment of love of neighbor? What manner of men had created this bloodthirsty God?

God, no doubt, was desperate. He must break into history. Man, being so blind, must have an example. After the centuries of this revengeful God who slaughtered little children, he had to come with a New Covenant and He, himself, would show us the cruelty of Elisha and the latent cruelty in us all. That's what the Incarnation is all about—God became one of us, showing us what love can do. The Old Covenant's law is displaced; it cannot be kept. The New Covenant of love can save us from ourselves and send us out for others. We no longer care too much about hair, or statue, or possessions, and no longer yearn for revenge.

Oh, that in this time of man's history, we as nations might not respond in curses and call out the she-bears to devour our children.

History

Hear what the New Covenant says in the parallel Gospels: "And they were bringing children to him that he might touch them; and the disciples rebuked them. But when Jesus saw it he was indignant and said to them, "Let the children come to me, do not hinder them; for to such belong the kingdom of God. 'Truly I say to you whoever does not receive the Kingdom of God like a child shall not enter it.' And he took them in his arms and blessed them, laying his hands upon them."

32

Come 2004 the Rossview Ladies' Aid will have spanned a century. What a dimension this band of ladies has added to Grace Chapel, Rossview. An ecumenical group, they have reached out to the total community in service, education, and above all, in true fellowship, that comes out of a society from bygone days when home entertainment was the norm.

What a dimension the Rossview Ladies' Aid added to Grace Chapel, Rossview.

History

The Ladies' Aid was organized April 23, 1904, by Mrs. John Ross who was the wife of Dr. John Ross, a brother to Captain Edward Barker Ross, Dr. Ted and John Ross's father. This Dr. Ross came into the community, along with his wife, to further education for his nieces and nephews and other deserving young persons in the neighborhood. Clara, his wife, did not forget the women who needed to broaden their outlook away from Rossview. She had a literary turn and felt the need for the Grace Chapel ladies being informed of the world situation—India in particular—and they began the study of that country and the mission work that could be done there. The ladies met for the first time at the home of the J. P. Killebrews, grandparents of Joe, Alf, Meta, and Gretchen Killebrew.

"It was decided that, as the funds would go to Grace Chapel, only the ladies of the Episcopal Church should pay dues—ten cents per month—and all the rest of the ladies of the community be invited to join as honorary members to study with us." So read their first minutes. Mrs. Clara Ross gave the first program, tracing the history of the Indian nation.

Mrs. Emily Fry Marshall, my husband's grandmother, was the first vice-president of the Ladies' Aid Society; and when in February, 1921, Emily's son, J. P. Marshall, brought his bride, Mary Beaumont, into the household, this organization would have a spark plug, a dynamo, that would make it go whether it wanted to or not. Mary never took "No" for an answer. All quilts must be made, all layettes finished, tickets sold to all benefits, and whatever happened, the Ladies' Aid Picnic must be held in August! The Bishop of Rossview had spoken.

History

33

Do not be conformed to this world but be transformed by the renewal of your mind that you may prove what is the will of God, what is good and acceptable and perfect.

Romans 12

This summer my need for green tomatoes renewed my mind, taking it back some five centuries to the Protestant Reformation. For the first time in some 50 years of housekeeping and pickle making, I had no green tomatoes for my family's favorite relish that goes on dried beans and in Mama's Perfect Potato Salad. This relish is our son's only requested Christmas present. Santa Claus was in crisis. What to do?

The original recipe called for a "water bucket of green tomatoes," and since drought had dried up all local gardens, I was referred to the Mennonites at Fairview, Ky., who, by God's grace, had a goodly supply of this basic ingredient. With Jefferson Davis's obelisk as a landmark, I made my way through Pembroke to Fairview where Joseph Zimmerman raised produce to sell.

Joseph was a reformation for me, giving me a glimpse into the transformation of ones totally committed to the will of God as they understood it. His spirit communicated a tenderness, a goodness, a quiet peacefulness that radiated from his face. His homemade garments seemed substituted for a woven, seamless robe and his rough shoes for well-trodden sandals. To add to his noble mien was his command of the English language and his well-modulated voice, far removed from the Southern Kentucky vernacular, spoken as though he had been instructed in a message from another time and place. No doubt his speech was that of his Pennsylvania brethren. There was sophistication in the bucolic boundaries of his place.

His place was a small roadside fruit and vegetable stand which he and his 12-year-old son, Jacob, were manning. There were plenty of ripe tomatoes, but no green ones. When I explained my dire

History

need for a water bucket of green tomatoes, Joseph brought Jacob into the discussion; and they decided after a father-son conference that Jacob would go back to the garden, some half mile away, to gather them. Knowing that the Mennonites eschewed riding in automobiles, I hesitated a moment but then volunteered to drive Jacob to the garden. Joseph agreed this arrangement was all right.

Jacob ran every step of the way through this task, his pantaloons waving and his straight straw hat bobbing while his bare feet ignored rocks and briars. In a few minutes he had my tomatoes ready to go. His eagerness to help and his delight in his work were a novelty in this day and age.

When we returned, Joseph, again, took his son into consultation, asking him how much he thought his work and the tomatoes were worth. After some pondering and looking at his father with proud eyes, he answered, "I guess a dollar." A dollar for a peck of green tomatoes! Joseph held with his son's price. But I couldn't hold it and told Jacob he had run at least a dollar's worth. They added four cucumbers to this bargain.

These Anabaptists were followers of Menno Simmons, a Dutch Reformist—therefore the name Mennonite. He was born in 1492 which tells us how long Joseph Zimmerman's forebears have struggled to keep their simple life transformed from the world. They refused to take up the sword, rejected infant baptism, did not swear oaths, were extreme individualists with each having the right to follow the dictates of his own conscience, denied the necessity of clergy with each person his own priest, responsible only to God. They lived communally and denounced the accumulation of wealth and taught the complete separation of church and state.

The "Plain People" abhorred the hierarchy of Rome with its bejeweled crowns and vestments and the lax living at this time of the Catholic clergy throughout Europe. Their reformation was a radical one, much more pronounced than Martin Luther's. Today we see these Anabaptists as Mennonite, Baptist and Pentecostal churches, each with its own interpretation of the literal word—the Bible. They were persecuted, run from country to country, yet they refused to live by the sword. Religious toleration in Canada and Pennsylvania brought them to the New World, where I find them in 2005, my neighbors, with green tomatoes.

Joseph Zimmerman's beatific face sent my mind reeling back some 500 years, mulling over my transformation and the renewing of my mind and my search for the good, the acceptable, and the perfect. When I stood in Joseph's presence, I felt as though I had lost my way, and I wonder if our established churches haven't wandered also. Have we conformed to the world and lost the simple gospel of Christ's unconditional love, depending more on our own piety and outworn dogmas and legalisms?

Let us search to renew our minds. Let us abandon our need to be "right." Let us yearn for our oneness in Christ. Let the good news of God's love for all resound anew.

The green tomato relish is in its jars. "God's in his heaven" and all's right in my pantry. Santa Claus will come.

34

When God said, "Let there be light," Franklin Delano Roosevelt heard him. He had a New Deal. What rejoicing there was in the rural South when the Tennessee Valley Authority strung its mighty lines across our countryside, delivering us from dreariness and drudgery. What a light shone in our darkness!

It was 1939, the year I was a junior at Clarksville High School, when the electricity was finally turned on. We were ready. The Frigidaire, as we called all refrigerators, was in place in the kitchen; a radio sat with great expectations; light globes were anticipating from the ceilings; an electric stove was impatient on the back porch; the wash board and the wash pots were cowering in the wash shed, awaiting their doomsday; but our old Rayo study lamp still reigned on the kitchen table where my brother and I did our homework in the winter by the Home Comfort stove. Coming

History

was the promise of no more wood chopping and filling the wood box on snowy days, and no more squinting at prepositional phrases and algebraic equations by our kerosene lamp. Praise be to TVA. ***ALLELUIA.***

One late winter afternoon when we had gotten home from school, a miracle had taken place. The house was humming. Mama already had ice cream freezing in the trays of the refrigerator. It was a bit icy, but tasted to us children like the ambrosia of the gods. Radio music filled the kitchen and the back porch and the ever-dark back hall were ablaze with light. Daddy, the most dedicated of sports fans, began to twist the dial for ballgames, not to mention the search for the weather and the latest news.

Of all the thankfulness for this liberating new day, my mother was the most joyous. Right away, she got a Maytag washing machine, one with a big tub and rollers to wring out the cloths as they passed through two rinses. On Monday mornings, using her magic water heater, she filled the tub, as its rhythmic agitating seemed to calm her as she hummed along and probably let the machine run too long. What sweet music. There were no timers or dryers, but most bright days found my mother having some excuse to put something on the line—a dirty rug or a tattered blanket or cloth feed bags.

Yet another washday celebration: an electric iron. No more soot on the ironing—just plug in this hot number, clean and smooth, and slick-iron all starched garments, and press all sheets and cup towels. How about that! "Water, water everywhere," but how difficult to get a drink. We had a dug well with chain and bucket and a smaller well with a hand pump. Can you envision what an electric pump meant for water in the house and a bathroom? This was the ultimate liberation. With the coming of rural electrification, our privy was overgrown with trumpet vine and honeysuckle until it finally collapsed into its pit. When the tomato vines grew too close to this spot, I wondered about those luscious tomatoes with their vines' wandering roots.

A portion of the back porch became our bathroom—a real bathroom with tub, hot and cold running water and a flushing commode. That was luxury unlimited. There were always grandchildren around, always craving to splash in the bathtub and enjoy the miracles of this new day. The toilet handle made for much rushing water and fountains of laughter, and what toddler cared about "no, no"?

There were negative opinions and unexpected results from this New Deal. Our neighbor across the road vowed that electric fans were the Devil's own invention, causing "rheumatiz and lumbago" from cooling back and forth with the resulting locked joints. My daddy, being an inventor, decided to electrify our Daisy churn. This unique churn had a cranking wheel and wooden lids atop a five-gallon square can. Someone gave him a one-horse power motor, which he mounted on a rolling platform and attached a drive belt to Daisy's ancient flywheel. When TVA grabbed Daisy, she took off in a wild dance, threw off her lids, splattered buttermilk in wild abandon to walls and ceiling, blinded our eyes and loosened all the soldering in her seams. Finally someone's shocked brains awoke and unplugged Daisy. She never danced again.

I, having been born in 1923 and lived through the Great Depression, FDR's New Deal, World War II and the present hour, have seen many deals. In our nation, we need a new, New Deal, one to light our way through these dark days of war and worldwide change. May we who walk in darkness see a great light.

35

Woe unto me that join house to house, that lay field to field, till there be no place.

Isaiah 5:8

My grandmother, Martha Elizabeth Winn, daughter of Thomas Jefferson Winn of Rudolphtown, was widowed at 20. Her husband, Greene Burnham Oliver, died from "consumption," leaving behind

History

my infant father. It was back to Grandpaw Winn's house. When my father was 8 years old, my grandmother married her husband's brother, one Isaac Oliver, down from Louisville with no land and no prospects. Mattie, as she was called, had come down in the world and was much maligned for remarrying, thanks to St. Paul.

My daddy was devoted to his stepfather, Uncle Ike. Uncle Ike found a tenant farmer situation on the Warfield Plantation where you travel now along Warfield Boulevard. He must have done well, because he managed to buy property at Kirkwood, a portion of the land from the famed Judge Tyler of Hickory Wild.

To make a short story longer, when my father was about 17, Uncle Ike died of "stomach problems," probably colon cancer, leaving Daddy head of the household and in care of my grandmother. There was only a log cabin on the farm there at Kirkwood, no home to make Grandmother proud; and ever being one to come up with remedies and ideas, my father determined to build her a home so she could hold her head high. He had to seek his fortune. At what point my father decided to go "north" I don't know, but he left for Pittsburgh where he heard there were jobs in the steel industry. Having fallen on a stubble as a child, he was blind in one eye and couldn't handle "high iron," but found a job as a clerk and bookkeeper in a mental institution. What tales he could tell.

Daddy saved his money until he could come home and build his mother a house. It was in this house I was reared. To make the house unique for Kirkwood, he ordered much of it from the Sears-Roebuck catalog—the tiled fireplaces and mirrored mantels, the colonnade, transom doors and doors that would swing both ways and a front door with a built-in bell. There was a railway switch at Hampton Station where all these appointments came in on a boxcar. What elegance! What joy for my grandmother.

In 1917, at 37, Daddy found time to get married, and he married an orphan girl who also had never had a home. Grandmother declared two women couldn't share the same man. She, being a flirt and full of fun, began courting in her 50s, and married the only grandfather I ever knew and moved to Clarksville, leaving her house to my mother and her three stair-step grandchildren—I, the youngest of three, was born in 1923.

We made full use of her house. We polished the upstairs banister with our behinds, hid in every attic and "dirty clothes" closet for hide-and-seek, tossed balls over the roof for "Annie Over," splashed in tin tubs by the kitchen stove and on state occasions had manners in the parlor and dining room. How cold these rooms were in winter.

The fancy fireplaces could barely take the chill off these rooms, not to mention the upstairs bedrooms. In the summer we lolled on the L-shaped front porch, pumping the swing back and forth while Daddy read the paper and spit, propping his feet on the nearest column. The screened-in back porch was the domestic hub of the household—churning, cream separating, chicken plucking, bean snapping, corn shucking and, in summer, ice cream-cranking. Grandmother's house was in full use until our mother could no longer take care of herself. She lived her last years with my husband and me and died in 1987 at 95. Thank you, Grandmother, for the use of your most treasured house.

Time marches on. "Progress" is upon us. Developers are scouting every square inch of Kirkwood land, much of it already sold and cleared of mighty oaks from Hampton Station to Kirkwood, on to Rossview and to Port Royal. Grandmother's house still stands. Behind us the old Tyler home, with its Hickory Wild Academy, has been torn down and built over, and no trace of the family cemetery is left. As a child, I played on this spot with its weathered early 1800 markers, one bricked tomb above ground and a grand towering obelisk.

Where did they go? No one knows.

My brother and I still own Grandmother's house. After we are gone and its final judgment meted out, it will no doubt go to the highest bidder and turned into the highest dollar. Its true value is beyond price.

History

36

Within this awful volume lies the mystery of mysteries!...

Sir Walter Scott

Censorship! Some books are too dirty to read. In this present debauched age, we must have it! There is one book in particular that records rape and incest, sexual harassment, deception and lies, wife swapping, nude dancing, genocide, pre-meditated murder and voluptuous perversions to titillate every imagination. Yet this book is handed out to people "joining the church," to graduates, to married couples, to newly confirmed communicants; and the Gideons spend most of their contributions placing a copy of this book in all hotel and motel rooms. Year after year, this volume tops all bestseller lists and has been translated into thousands of languages. This is the Word of the Lord—the Bible. What is the mystery and the might of this book?

This God of Abraham, Isaac and Jacob has caused His word to be set down, not glossed over, but showing man in all his humanity, letting it be known that there is nothing new under the sun and that all are Adam and Eve's fallen children.

Abraham, the first called-out Patriarch, began the story of God's chosen people. He was obedient to God's call to leave his country with his beautiful wife, Sarah. Right away he became a liar when he came to the land of Egypt where he saved himself by saying that Sarah was his sister. Pharaoh took Sarah into his household for his wife, and to make matters worse for Pharaoh, the Lord afflicted him because of Abraham's lies. That doesn't seem fair. When they settled in their tents, Sarah stirred up more trouble when she gave her slave girl, Hagar, to Abraham to have his child. Substitute mothers are nothing new. When Sarah laughed at God about becoming pregnant in her old age, God showed her who was God, and she became the mother of Isaac. Poor Hagar and her son

History

Ishmael were cast out in the desert. To this very hour, Ishmael's and Isaac's descendants are killing each other over their inheritance from Abraham.

Incest is recorded in the 19th chapter of Genesis. This sin, along with lies and deceptions, is as old as the scriptures. After Lot and his two daughters were saved from the destruction of Sodom and Gomorrah—the cities of rampant homosexuality—the daughters decided their father was the last living male on earth. To preserve posterity, he got Lot drunk (Ah, the evils of alcohol) and both became pregnant by their father. This is tabloid stuff. Don't let your children read this chapter, and certainly don't let this story out in Sunday school.

One of the best lessons we had in our Baptist Sunday School was the story of Jacob and Esau, Isaac's twin sons. Esau was born first, which gave him the blessing, the birthright. Their mother, Rebekah, was partial to Jacob, and when the blessing was given, she disguised Jacob in Esau's clothing and put a lambskin on his body, for Esau was a hairy man. Being blind, old Isaac gave the blessing to the wrong son, causing Esau to vow to kill his brother. Lies and deception again.

The stories go on and on: Jacob cheats his father-in-law, Laban; Jacob's daughter, Dinah, is seduced; Jacob's revenge by mass slaughter; Joseph's brothers sell him into slavery. Thus reads the history of the Patriarchs.

Probably the best example of X-rated material is found in David's story—the man after God's own heart. When the Ark of the Covenant was brought to Jerusalem, David became so excited with shouting and dancing that he danced naked before the Ark and exposed himself "before the eyes of his servant maids." One of his wives upbraided him for this nude dance and he replied, "I will make merry before the Lord; I will make myself yet more contemptible than this..." No henpecked husband David. Too bad he didn't have a G-string for tucking away tips.

History

How many wives and concubines did David have? God only knew—and David wanted more. When he saw the beautiful Bathsheba at her bath, he sent her husband into the front line of the army so he would be killed. Bathsheba was the mother of Solomon, who followed David as king over Israel. When, at the end of his life, David was sick and cold, his servants looked the countryside over for a young virgin, beautiful beyond description, to "lie in his bosom" and warm him. Even with the servants' efforts and the tender care of the young maiden, the King James Version states "the king gat no heat."

The stories go on to Solomon and his many wives and concubines, Samson in the fleshpots of Egypt, and continue yet into the contemporary news of our times. The stories haven't changed—just the cast of characters.

Our parallels to these several-thousand-year-old stories should bring us comfort. There is nothing new under the sun, no new sin to shock the Almighty, no perversion that is not recorded in the story of his people, no depth of cruelty or genocide that is left out, no infidelity that is not in the record.

If we only had the Old Testament, the Pentateuch in particular, it would probably be more consistent to call these first five books of the Bible the word of the demonic, rather than the Word of God. The evolution of the Vengeful God to the loving Father God took many a century, David being one of the first sweet singers to this God. The prophet Isaiah foretold the coming of the servant God, the one bruised for our iniquity, the one to take away the sins of the world.

When you read in The Leaf Chronicle the headlines about politicians with temptations like David's, greedy schemes for financial gain like Jacob's, rape and murder like in Dinah's story, get all this in perspective: This is the continuing record of man. This is our story.

In the New Testament we have a new story, however—a new hope in Christ. He is the way to peace that calls us to rise above all the tumult of earthly conflict and tragedy. Even though we have known every sin of the Old Testament, through Christ we are forgiven, and made clean and will be made like him. This is the mystery of the Word of God made flesh.

History

KIRKWOOD

37

The love of money and the love of learning rarely meet.

George Herbert

"Why, when I was at Kirkwood School, a million dollars would have educated the State of Tennessee. What is this all about buses, consolidation, sports programs, special education and different tracks, art and music, and in-service for teachers? . . . A bunch of tom-foolery! A couple of rooms, a chalk board, a teacher with a good head and a tough hide, and some knot head pupils—that's all you need." Thus went the commentary of an old friend.

This knot head lived in sight of Kirkwood school's two rooms. Later on when the enrollment went up, a third room was added with a portable partition and behind this was built a stage, a board worthy of our Thespian efforts at Halloween and Christmas. It was beside this stage on the other side of the partition that I had special education with a special educator. For me, love of learning began, and there was no money involved.

The school's rooms were furnished with single and double desks, and if you were of certain deportment—didn't poke ribs, talk too much, chew tobacco in class, or pass dirty notes—you could share a double desk on the other side of the partition. Being threatened by my mother with violence for misbehavior, I was one of the favored ones. Lucky for me, one Keith Powers, the third son of Miss Gloria Powers of the "True Eye," took me as his protégée; there, I had a private tutor as we shared a double desk away from the other four classes in our crowded room.

Long division was a mystery to my non-mathematical mind. With the utmost patience, this gangling fourteen-year-old boy, wise and wonderful in my eyes, took me step-by-step through division problems as only a master teacher could do. From Miss Gloria's example, Keith gloried in reading. After our math lesson was finished, he would choose a book for each of us from the library-on-wheels where we lost ourselves in the worlds of King Arthur, the Swamp Fox, and Tom Sawyer. Often the teacher forgot to call us when our class's turn came to go up front to recite. To Keith, across the years, I give the highest acclaim to one who taught me how to study and how to travel into new realms.

During these depression years, there was no money to love. But love of school and the love of creating our extracurricular activities kept us charmed. As near as I was to the schoolhouse, I refused to go home at noon for lunch but wolfed down sausage biscuits and fried-egg sandwiches lest I miss the first inning of the baseball game. We played with home-wound, string balls and soap paddle bats. The PTA sacrificed its entire treasury for a basketball, which brought on a flurry of activity: scraping the school grounds for a court, building the backboards, and salvaging hoops from the community's junk piles. We lived in Tarzan's jungle, swinging down long saplings in the bordering woods while practicing whatever ape-related yells and melodies we felt in our bones. With long poles, we high-vaulted wet weather branches for "Cross the Atlantic" and sent the law after Bonnie and Clyde until Bonnie took refuge in the privy and fell through the floor. Graciously, the WPA furnished us with two sanitary "government" toilets.

There were no buses; we walked to school. There was no remedial reading. If you couldn't learn to read, you went home to farm or to "help Mama." We read the Bible every day, said the Lord's Prayer, and saluted the flag. There were no protests or lawsuits. Dr. Malone came once a year for shots and that was our health care. There was an administration of one—Professor Jobe, as we called him, a scholarly man who was interested in all aspects of our rural education. His legacy lives on in his descendants. Mary Jo Winters, his granddaughter, from her family of fourteen children, has eight who follow their great-grandfather's footsteps.

Our innocent age had no inkling of the unimaginable upheavals awaiting it at the close of this century. Our OK Tablets and chalkboards are lost in the revolution of the computer age. There is now money, and to be honest, we love it. Luxuries unheard of are ours. The love of learning has been in many instances endowed by this money so that the twain seem to have met. Upon his death, a good friend so endowed Austin Peay State University because he loved his home community and the people who made his inheritance possible.

The constructive use of money, as in the parable of the talents, is our duty. Rather than a narrow hoarding and worshiping of wealth, we are called on to love its use for our families' welfare, for the education of the community, for the larger purposes of our nation. For sure, we will not take one thin dime when we die.

Therefore, those whose destructive use of money compel them to hoard it and worship at its feet shall lose it; but those who give it away for their neighbor's sake shall have it returned, heaped-up with joy, to keep for eternity.

38

Thou shalt not be afraid of the terror by night; nor the arrow that flieth by day.

Psalm 91

Our dark tobacco barn was mightily fired in October. In the late evening, the long ribbons of smoke would wend their way through the golden air, settle their pungent incense over the orchard and garden and settle eerily into the pumpkin patch by the hog pen. The lingering smoke carried us children into a realm of hobgoblins that grew in anticipation of Halloween; and we had two grand black men in our barn who could have won the Ichabod Crane Award.

George Killebrew and Thomas Moody, late of Kirkwood, were the keepers of the curing fires which had to be tended all night lest they flame up and burn the barn down. At dusk Mama placed

George and Thomas's supper in a big stew pot with a wire bail and a lid held in place by a dangling clamp and chain. Into this pot Mama placed all manner of hungry-man food which usually included pie, "because Thomas is partial to pie." Then my brother or I, or sometimes both, were sent down the lane to the inferno of smoke and fiery fiends.

As you opened the barn door and the acrid smoke and heat overwhelmed your senses, you could not see until your eyes cleared a bit and you found airspace in which to breathe. The sawdust and backlogs, flaming and sparking, hid George and Thomas until we at length made them out sitting in hickory split chairs propped against a wall where there was a breathing space. Carefully, we crimpled our feet like firewalkers until we put their supper down on a sawhorse table. At once the evening's fun began.

"My, my, I sure can tell you had pie for supper. Come here, boy, let me lick around your mouth so I can taste that pie." George always greeted us with this idle threat. My brother and I loved him with a special love that in this day of political correctness would not be understood. He was one of the rocks of our childhood. Uncle Thomas was quite austere, but he was a master storyteller who through the smoke and fear of the dark took us on wings of fright through ghostly suicides of years past and unsolved apparitions in his church's graveyard.

Across the road from our house was the old Marshall place, belonging to forgotten relatives of my husband's family. After the Civil War, so the story goes, a woman in the family hanged herself in the attic room in this rambling old farmhouse. We children would creep up the steps in this remote part of the house and stare at a cut-off rope, reputed to be the very rope by which the woman garroted herself. In July in broad open daylight, this was scary stuff. In October with Halloween coming and Uncle Thomas embellishing every detail, this old house in the smoke and dark was indeed a terror by night.

"Every night I can look through this crack in the barn and there her haint is. Her long dress is tangled up in the smoke but her eyes is red and you can hear her moanin'. She's cryin' for the man who got hisself blowed away in the war. Comes out every night just before the moon when it's moon time. That's when she's plainest. You look good when you shut the door outside. Y'all see her for sure."

My brother tells best his return home, alone, from the barn to the back porch. "As soon as I shut the door to the outside, I would take a deep fresh air breath and step around the corner of the barn. George and Thomas were still laughing inside and there was nothing except lots of smoke curling from under the roof. Nothing to be afraid of. The clamp and the chain on the stew pot clanged on the side, and as I picked up speed the lid started to chatter. The faster I ran the more the pot clanged and the lid chattered. Through a knothole in the barn came long wailing moans and the woman's white dress would cross my face as I felt her dark-fired breath on the back of my neck. Just before the terror grabbed me, the lamp in the kitchen window chased the haint back into the smoke as I redesigned the back screen door."

The years, however, have not taken our fears and anxieties away. We have exchanged childish fears for more awesome ones. There are still terrors by night and arrows by day. There is the confusion called living—our fears for our health, our death, our children and the safety of the world. Unknown arrows can fly by night and day and terrors can be made beyond all imagination. Our hope is in the "peace that passeth all understanding" and the "perfect love that casts out all fear." May this peace and love be our ever-present help from the Power beyond all human knowing.

39

I love him because he's wonderful
Because he's just plain Bill.

Rodgers & Hammerstein

In the book of Genesis, it is recorded that there were giants in the earth in those days. I contend they are here yet, and I knew a wonderful one whose name was Bill—our own Bill McCraw—late of Kirkwood.

On April 1, 2001, we who loved him came together at his funeral to tell of our past years' remembrances, to recall the many funny "Bill" stories, and to bid him Godspeed to a place of perpetual benediction. His great heart and body and his native goodness made no funeral oration necessary. Bill's life had spoken and continues to speak.

Maggie and Logan McCraw seemed to have been called to produce four stalwart men, men the whole countryside would rise up and call blessed because of their love of life and their love of neighbor. There were Turner, Joe, Lynn, and lastly, Bill. Bill was the one my infant years knew best because he was the protector of my brother and me at Kirkwood School where there was no such thing as supervised play. No one picked on us. Bill was there. He was about six years older than I, which made him about 13 or 14. Already at this age, he was a formidable protector, already 6 feet tall with muscles filled out from wrestling mules and eating at Maggie McCraw's bountiful table. In the morning she would ask Bill, "Do you want a whole-fry or a half-fry?" which meant a dozen eggs or a half-dozen. To add to this was a pan of biscuits and a platter of fried, smoked shoulder. His appetite matched his muscles, and Mrs. McCraw reveled in these statistics. Her Bill did no wrong.

Back to the playground. When Bill came on the scene, order reigned. There was no cheating, no name calling, no batting out of turn, no put-down of unfortunate children in their poor clothing in those Depression days. His was an innate sense of fairness and empathy for the little children and the ones on the fringe of survival. How excellent to have had a giant's strength and to have used it so gently and graciously.

Bill had a decided impediment in his speech that somehow made him most winsome and huggable. Never once did he seem self-conscious, and he was famous as a raconteur, his stories legendary in Kirkwood folklore. His unique speech patterns made his stories enthralling; and they linger, yet, indelible in our memory. At a gathering in our later years, these gems were requested and told, and retold. Bill enjoyed them most of all.

My brother's name is Woodson and the best Bill could ever say his name was Woosa. Woosa's favorite "Bill" story was "Flipping for Possum Hides." With apologies to Bill, I recount this story as best I remember it.

"During the 'Pression, a dime look like a wagon wheel. I read in paper that Mr. Heimanson paying good money for possum hide and I had old Ruff, the best possum dog in Montgomery County. We gonna get rich. Dog and I went huntin' every night, all night long, 'til I finally had about two hundred possum hide stretch out on smokehouse wall. One night some already-caught possums got away and we had to hunt them down again. Pore dog got worked so hard he died in back of truck. I hate killin' a good dog. He didn't get nothin' for his work. When the huntin' was over, I took hides to town down to Mr. Heimanson. He say the market glutted and he can give me one cent per hide. Two dollars for two hundred possum hides! So I say to him, 'I flip you, double or nothing.' Mr. Heimanson, he win. All I got out this deal was a dead dog, and no sleep for six months. But I did get trip to town."

One of the Proverbs read: He that is of a merry heart has a continual feast—and never was I in Bill's presence that he didn't show his merry heart and his mastery of good humor.

He was just plain Bill but there was an elegance, an assurance, that was quiet, but spoke volumes about who he was. He wore a mantle of respect from friends and family—all. He was one who could laugh at himself, but not at anyone else. He was one that if you needed to cry, he would be there, listening. If you needed strength, either physical or psychical, he was there to bolster you. He knew that strength is made perfect in weakness.

Maggie and Logan McCraw doted on their Bill, and rightly so. So do his wife Elizabeth, his son and daughter, his grandchildren, and all of us who happened to fall under the tutelage of this colossus among men.

And we love him because he's wonderful. Because he's just our Bill.

40

The Montgomery County Historical Society invited me to speak about some chosen childhood recollections for their March 16th program. Therefore, I decided to kill two audiences with one story, more or less. Having been born in 1923, I have had plenty of time to recollect, and I chose to go way back, back to my earliest remembrances of my parents, our two-room school at Kirkwood, and our one-room Baptist church just across from the school.

What memories of my father, one Bracy Oliver. He was a jubilant heart with his funny bone always in operation, charming each new set of children who came to our little Baptist church. Ask Rubye Patch. He was born in 1880, sixteen years after the Civil War, and was truly of the horse-and-buggy generation, marveling at the end of his life at coming from this age to the walking-on-the-moon age with its explosion of technology. As a boy, his dream was to have a fine horse with a "buggy behind" as he liked to say. Just as the present-day boys and girls want a fast car or a pick-up truck, his passion was a sleek buggy horse to go courting. A-courtin' he did go. He drove his elegant rig to Palmyra, picked up Maude Livingston, stopped at some preacher's house for a wedding, and brought his bride to Kirkwood where the home of my childhood still stands.

The country roads that I first remember were just plain dirt and during the winter freezes-and-thaws were impassable. I, too, was of the horse-and-buggy era because in the winter our Model T Ford would not go through deep mud holes, finding Daddy getting out the buggy and hitching up Topsy. Well I remember a Christmas visit to Aunt Lena's—Mrs. Minor Randle, Evelyn Frost's mother—in the buggy. Snow began to fall as we went home. Not to worry. Daddy had a buggy lap rug, most scratchy with a tiger skin printed deep into the fur, and the tiger watched you with yellow glass eyes that threatened to scratch you to death or eat you up. This indeed is an early recollection.

Bracy Oliver was a jubilant heart with his funny bone always in operation.

Judge John T. Cunningham ran on a ticket of gravelling every county road if elected. He handily won and stuck with his campaign promise. I remember truck after truck lifting up its load and putting down an all-weather road in front of our house. Bless your memory, Judge Cunningham. Following his interest in roads, Montgomery County has paved every road in the county, even to the deepest ones in Owl Hollow. Few counties in Tennessee can match this record.

My parents had three children within three years—"just like popping corn" Mama said. From 1920 to 1923, my sister, my brother, then I, the youngest, were born. Daddy said that they finally found out what was causing all these children.

I do not remember starting to school. The two-room school, with vestibule for coats, galoshes, and sack lunches and complemented with a boys' and girls' privy in the back playground, was a few hundred yards from our home, so with some regularity I would slip off and follow my brother and sister.

Bless Miss Eleanor McCain, the first grade teacher. She let me come and I cannot remember learning to read, only remember her holding me on her lap and assuring my mother that my insistence on school was "all right." I was five in March and was legally enrolled in 1928. All our teachers, except one sourpuss, were veterans, well educated and dedicated to learning, giving us a foundation that under girds me yet. When I left the lower grades room and went to the higher room, what an education to hear the history and geography lessons when the 7th and 8th grades went up front to the recitation bench. There was an unspoken line at which some students' schooling was cut short. If by the 5th grade, students didn't know the multiplication tables and could not read with comprehension, they could quietly quit school and go home to help on the farm or, if female, learn to cook and sew at home. That's just the way it was.

Even though we lived almost in the school door, we wouldn't go home for lunch, stuffing sausage biscuits or whatever in a paper bag, wolfed the lunch down, for fear of missing the beginning of the ballgame or the marble shoot. We made up games, climbed trees in an adjacent woods, and poled over wet weather branches. When the "Fox and Hound" game got too hot and we girls were about to be caught, we made a mad dash to the privy. What recollections, and I did learn my tables and conquered the mystery of long division, thanks to the help of an 8th grade boy.

Church was my other acculturation. I do give thanks to the King James Version of Holy Scripture that I heard from infancy at Kirkwood Baptist Church. I have several translations, but when I want beauty and poetry, I read this flow of Elizabethan English. Then there was music—old Baptist hymns that I piped with much fervor standing on the wooden benches as Daddy sang a fine bass line. My love of music started here. The only minus for my tender years at our church was the eternal hellfire and damnation sermons. I had Hell scared into me. During the revival, I couldn't go to sleep because if I died in the night, I would wake up in Hell and burn forever and forever. "Let the little children come unto me for of such is the kingdom of heaven," I never heard.

Thanks be to God, there were liberators in our church, the main one I remember was Rubye Draughon Menees, Rubye Patch's grandmother. She was a foreigner from up around Springfield where they knew how to play cards, dance, and have a general good time. She lived with her son Robert and his wife Katherine Kennedy Menees, all loyal Baptists. When I was a teenager, Katherine was pregnant, and with our just being a little beyond the stork explanation, we were totally fascinated. Katherine produced twins: Rubye Draughon and Jimmy. They were fraternal twins; never could they have been in the same placenta with Rubye totally like her grandmother and Jimmy like the quiet Meneeses. Grandmother Menees would never join Kirkwood Church. She had creative ideas, much joy for living, and a wonderful wit with no patience for narrow dogmas. On closed communion Sundays, I think she stayed at home.

> *He who careth not from whence he came, careth little wither he goeth.*
>
> **Daniel Webster**

In the year 2009, after 86 years, I careth wither I go. I go as one who gives thanks for parents who truly cared for me, for what small knowledge I have learned along the way, and for the divine mystery of creation and for unconditional love that is the powerful force that we so dimly grasp. My caring is that we shall know this love.

41

> *How dear to my heart are the scenes of my childhood, when fond recollections present them to view.*
>
> **Samuel Wordworth's The Old Oaken Bucket**

As I grow old and older, the scenes of my childhood grow nearer and dearer, and fond recollections and sad reflections combine. "There is nothing permanent but change," but in our present day determination for wealth and "progress," much of the revered history of our past has been destroyed, covered up, trampled on, desecrated and forgotten.

Adjoining our farm was the old Hickory Wild Academy. My brother and I have not forgotten. On the line fence that separated the two farms, our farm being part of the original John Duke Tyler tract, was the family cemetery with dates on the stones back to the early 1800s, with one tomb walled up above ground, another, a tall obelisk for John Duke that seemed like the Washington Monument to my brother and me. There were many less grand tombstones, all protected by a wrought iron fence. On this spot just up from our stable, we played and wondered at the silent tombs, knowing somehow that we were on hallowed ground. As children, we were taught not to step on earth that held sacred bones. Now there is no trace of this family graveyard. No one knows; all is silence; gone where God only knows.

Who among us holds this secret of the dead, the destruction of the Tyler cemetery? I remember well the original Hickory Wild Academy building. There were tall stone steps that led up to the columned porch that boasted two grand doors that led into the front hall. Typically, there were four large rooms downstairs, two on each side of the hall. A stairway in the hall led up to the second story where some boarding students in times past had lived. There was dignified grandeur there; but from the fireplaces in each room, I could imagine the drafts from such large spaces to such small sources of heat.

When I first knew Hickory Wild, it had lost its academy status and had been divided into smaller tracts of land. It was home to a family of Powells, who many old-timers will remember. It was a big family. The ones I remember well were Porter Powell, Homer Powell, Bertha Murphy Powell, Sarah Powell Winn, and then another generation—Arthur Earl Powell, Porter's son, and his daughter, Judy Powell Landiss, along with Fred, a gift to Clarksville.

During the Great Depression, the country side was in economic turmoil, and Hickory Wild was sold. The new owners demolished the academy and replaced it with a four-room, concrete block house that stood until the farm was sold again to developers. Somewhere in this timeframe, the cemetery was destroyed. By whom is the mystery. The old owners knew nothing, the developers knew nothing, and all that I know is that this valuable piece of history is gone.

The local chapter of the Historical Society is named the Charles Waller Tyler Chapter. He was county judge from 1873 to 1918. He was the youngest son of John Duke Tyler, who was educated in Virginia as a brilliant classical scholar and brought his vast learning to Hickory Wild. There both Greek and Latin were taught and Charles had mastered both by age 15. Wow! Male students from near and far enrolled in this academy in District 1,

Kirkwood

Montgomery County, in the Kirkwood community. At one time there were as many as 40-plus students, among them my husband's grandfather, James Carter Marshall, a day student living nearby.

Charles' judgeship called him to Clarksville where he lived during his long term as county judge. He was not interred in the family plot at Hickory Wild but at Greenwood, where he had buried in 1885 his beloved 4-year-old daughter, Nannie. The bereaved father commissioned a life-sized sculpture in marble in her image to mark her grave. In 1996, she was stolen from Greenwood and showed up at an antique dealer's shop in Boston. Nannie had made the national papers, and the honorable dealer sent Nannie home, where to this hour she is garlanded with flowers and love and respect.

Not so for John Duke Tyler and his family, buried at Hickory Wild. During the transfer of the property from owner to developer, all was lost. I went there to see. I had told the members of the Historical Society that I knew exactly where to take them to see the cemetery and to record the information on the tombstones. Nothing. To destroy a cemetery is a criminal act.

Across the road from Hickory Wild, there is a rebirth of honor for this name. A new development, beginning on Dunlop Lane and going through to Kirkwood Road, is named for this old academy. At its center is a tower with a school bell to remind Montgomery County of classical learning in years gone by.

Nannie's kidnapping and return had a nationwide rejoicing. John Duke Tyler's obelisk is yet a mystery unsolved. Who is as honorable as Mr. Stephen Score of Boston, who had paid $2,500 for Nannie, yet returned her. Who is honorable enough to step forward and say, "I know where John Tyler's stone lies." That would be honor and courage indeed!

May eternal rest be with the Tyler family wherever they are placed away from Hickory Wild, and may unrest be in the hearts of the ones who took away these scenes of my early childhood.

42

We're eatin' high on the hog.

When Thanksgiving was over and the thermometer lowered toward Christmas, my daddy began to eye the sky. He must have some clear, chilling days—not freezing, but frosty—for an annual event. It was hog killing time. The word got out across the neighborhood: Bracy Oliver was setting his scalding tub, waiting for just the right spell for this mass hog slaughter.

All the neighbors had their pigs in the fattening pens, awaiting the word from my father when to come. The hog killing, integrated and ecumenical, brought together many families, all hungry for fresh meat, all longing for hog-heaven.

On the just-right-frosty-clear morning and long before daylight, Daddy lit the fire under the scalding kettle, which for many days had been filled with the proper amount of water. This tub was a long rectangle, deep enough to hold a huge hog and scald away his bristles and leave him white and clean. By sun up the water was boiling. Families with their doomed cargo in their wagons began to arrive, and here was the time I retreated to the house—the crack of a rifle bullet and then the slitting of the throats of each squealing hog was more than I could witness.

Great muscled men brought the carcasses to the scalding tub and wrestled with chains to submerge the bodies; and after the proper time to loosen the hair, dragged them out, scraped them clean, and hung them on the *gambelling* pole. We called this pole the "gambling pole," and with all the hazards of this day, "gambling" was probably the best name. The hogs were hung up by the tendons in their hind legs and were up high enough that their snouts did not touch the ground. Here is where the gore began. With a brutally sharpened knife, a talented butcher with one long sweeping stroke cascaded the entire viscera into a waiting tub. The entrails—the offal, according to the French—were hung on a fence, and this steaming mass was the source of our eating low-on-the-hog—the liver, the lungs, the heart, the pancreas, "all but the squeal." These were the ingredients for our hog-killing lunch, which was called "Pluck Stew." Maybe it took pluck to eat it!

Mama baked great pans of sweet potatoes in the Home Comfort range and all the crusty cornbread that this culinary delight needed. Don't ask me for the recipe for Pluck Stew. I just know that it was brown, full of onions, sage and hot pepper.

Day one was the slaughter, the blocking out of the meat into hams, bacon, shoulders, jowls, spare ribs and backbones. All was to be thoroughly chilled overnight. The trimmings were set aside for sausage and the leaf fat for lard rendering on the second day. Some ladies were busy with the chitterlings, cleaning and soaking them for a special treat that I never had the nerve to enjoy.

The second day was Mama's day. She would let no one render the lard. It must be snowy white. Giant iron kettles held the bubbling fat, and when it was just right, it was strained into five gallon lard stands. Cracklings were left over from the lard press and were much desired for crackling bread. On this second day, the sausage was ground and sacked and the souse was cooked. Souse was ears, pig feet, snouts and other questionable parts molded into a gelatinous, slicing delight. The trimmed meat was salted down in the smoke house for about three weeks, waiting to be hung up and smoked. Real smoked country ham is truly "high-on-the-hog."

Why do I recount these pig tales? It has been said that when you start living in the past that you are indeed getting old. Well, all right! I am old and I think the histories of our past are worth remembering. These accounts remind us that we are living in a new age of instant gratification and unimagined luxuries, where meat is packaged, eggs are in cartons and milk in plastic jugs.

After Adam's disobedience, God told him he would earn his living by the sweat of his brow. Now we are living in the age of "no sweat." Every luxury is at our fingertips, and I must admit that I am thankful that I'm not hog killing on this cold, windy day with smoke in my eyes. As an old fogey, I lament the loss of community, cherish the loving and helpful respect between the races at our home, and recall the thankfulness for our blessings. Yes, we took time to thank God for the Pluck Stew in the iron pot and for our sense of pride in a powerful job, well-done.

Christ pronounced all that God had created as "clean." Peter, a devout Jew, who followed all the dietary laws, was told in a vision to eat all sorts of unclean animals and reptiles. "What God has cleansed, you must not call common and unclean." Thank you, Lord, for the lowly pigs who do root mightily in the dirt and for us Gentiles who were included in Peter's vision, and we were pronounced uncommon and clean and "grafted in" as your chosen people.

So, dear brothers and sisters, let us not be pigheaded, but accept all creation as good and all peoples as God's own. Thank you doubly, lowly pigs, for giving your lives so we can eat "high-on-the-hog."

MAMA AND DADDY

43

Kirkwood has known Greek and Latin, both spoken and written. I remember the remnants of the Hickory Wild Academy, a boarding school for young gentlemen, where in 1865, James Carter Marshall, Jack's grandfather, was a student. He was the son of Horace Dudley Marshall, the family who gave the land for Kirkwood Church. Being just across the road from Hickory Wild, young James Carter was not a boarding student. James Carter Marshall became a young doctor who practiced in Guthrie, Kentucky. He died in 1899. The academy was behind the site of the old Kirkwood School and adjoined the backside of my parents' farm.

Tidewater culture was transported to Hampton Springs, later Hampton Station, and in 1831, found its final destination on the Tyler farm at Kirkwood. John Duke Tyler, son of Richard Keeling Tyler, was born in Virginia in 1794 and was the founder of Hickory Wild. Both Richard and his son, John, were classical scholars known throughout the South with John Duke far outstripping his father as he never gave up his quest for deeper knowledge in all disciplines. They were lovers of life—masters of the violin, adept at dancing the minuet, readers of poetry and drama, and planners of great house parties that lasted for some days.

I knew Hickory Wild as a home for the Elisha Davis Powell family. My father, as a young man, was great friends with the Powell boys with much fun and devilment swapped across the fence. Such fun my father recounted from their doings, among them a collection of parlor tricks and other scandals. Gone were the days of Greek and Latin.

44

To be perpetually talking sense runs out the mind, as perpetually ploughing and taking out crops runs out the land. The mind must be manured, and nonsense is very good for the purpose.

James Boswell 1740-1795

My father, Bracy Oliver, looked forward to the nonsense of April Fool's Day, revering it like Independence Day. In his soul there was a nobility of nonsense, springing, perhaps from some merry ancestor's recessive gene. Fun and foolishness were ever foremost in his plans for daily living. Generations of Kirkwood inhabitants recount until this hour—if they be more than fifty years—some bucolic merriment of his making. There were string tricks, riddles, mumble-peg bouts, rolley-holley, annie-over, corncob wars in the hayloft; and best of all, around April Fool's Day, parlor games and tricks.

In this day of instant, push-button entertainment, parlor games will be difficult to envision. But we made our fun from "Spin-the-Bottle" to "Musical Chairs" to my father's favorite trick—"Going to Heaven."

"Going to Heaven" depended on a new boy or boys coming into the community who hadn't been to heaven. This trip called for elaborate plans. My father chose three pretty girls to guide these souls to paradise. Three straight chairs were lined up, a heavy quilt draped over the back of the chairs, the three girls were placed behind each of the three degrees of heaven, and my father crouched, hidden, behind these heavenly guides.

Already in the parlor were the guests who were in-the-know about this trick. The unsuspecting boys were kept out of the room until all was ready and then they were called in, one by one. They sized up the three pretty girls and were asked, "Do you want to go to heaven? Are you ready for the first degree?" With a "yes" answer they were blindfolded and sat in the first chair at which time my father popped from behind his hiding place and gave the poor boy a big kiss on the cheek. With this, there were cheers and whistles from the audience and the victim was asked if he were ready for the second degree. Usually he was. There was a longer and more lingering kiss which called for the third degree, and even longer and louder smackeroos. If there were more boys to go to heaven, the first was unblindfolded to watch his compatriots get kissed by an ugly old man rather than the pretty girls.

The "Stuck-Up-Society" was trotted out for newcomers of both sexes. My father presented this as some exclusive society, one which banned all riff-raff and only included persons of aristocratic blood and traceable ancestry back to the founding fathers or some personage of nobility. What a spiel he gave! After the introduction and the verification that they totally and truly wanted to join this exclusive society, he asked them to kneel for the oath. The swearing-in began. "Repeat after me—'I believe with all my heart'—a long pause—'I believe with all my mind.' At this point the initiates were asked to put their foreheads down to the floor as my father in his most stentorian tones asked them again to repeat after him—'I believe that I am'—long pause—'Stuck up behind!'"

Mama thought this one too much for polite society; however, Daddy did not rest until he initiated one woman, the community queen of up-tightness, into the Society. Rather than hitting him with her umbrella, her face unfroze in a moment of self-realization when nonsense overcame her perpetual pride in being proper and forever having her senses under control.

My father's parlor tricks are a study in the pursuit of our true selves, into our need for love and acceptance. Who among us as a teenager did not dream of being kissed, even blindfolded by our passions, by some idol in the neighborhood or perhaps in the movies? God in his grace gave us the need for romantic love to perpetuate the race and to prepare us for a deeper understanding of self-giving as we grow older. Nonsense along the way can add to our good sense of what is right and true and just and can ease the burden of everyday living. Remember the Proverb about laughter being the best medicine?

Mama and Daddy

We have all joined the "Stuck-up Society." Trying to bolster our fragile egos, we pretend, we buy more "stuff," we suck-up to the ones we think have arrived, we trace our ancestry back to some remote tale of family greatness, we create facades of beauty and culture. All the while being too serious about all this to take time to manure our brains—our poor depleted brains. Let us nourish them with laughter.

__Singing in the Rain. Let us nourish our brains with laughter.__

45

Pride goeth before destruction and a haughty spirit before a fall.

Proverbs 16:18

As Groundhog Day approaches and St. Valentine's Day follows, what folly can I report while still in the ice and snow of January! Groundhogs and hearts and flowers are such disparate subjects that they leave me in January, musing back some 55 years to a time of my deluded invincibility and my father's faulty faith that I could do all things—the pride that goes before destruction.

I was my father's other boy. At 13, tall, big-footed and prematurely grown, I could wrestle my just older brother to the ground any day and outrun him in any race. When he got his teenage growth at 16, my haughty spirit took its fall; however, my father never doubted my prowess, even into adulthood.

In January 1951, I was called on to show my mettle. On a severely cold day, treacherously glazed with ice and snow, Daddy had a load of tobacco in the barn that needed to be gotten out to the highway to be taken to market. Unless it was towed down the snowbound lane, the truck load of tobacco couldn't be gotten out. His answer: Charlotte!

My husband Jack was still at sea after WW II, and I was staying with Mama and Daddy until he came home, and we could move to our new farm on Pollard Road. Being ever the farmer, on land or at sea, he had bought a new, beautifully green John Deere G tractor—the love of his life, after me, I hope—which was stored in Daddy's barn. "Ah ha, a tractor, a driver, and we're out of here," reasoned my father, never considering my inexperienced tractor-driving.

Now most of you Gentle Readers have no idea of an old John Deere G, a model that had a hand clutch that had to be persuaded in-and-out as it made its "POP, POP, POP, POPS" on two cylinders. To compound the problem with this recalcitrant clutch was the fact of the cold weather and this device's little use. Destruction was in the offing—but I could do all things.

Before this tale progresses further, you must be informed that I was newly pregnant with Charles, our older son, who was born in August, 1951.

Down to the barn Daddy and I go and finally got the G warmed up enough to start. I got the clutch in reverse, backed out of the barn, Daddy fastened the chain to the truck, and away we went out to the main road. Everything was fine except my frozen hands and feet—and the clutch.

With the job finished, Daddy went to the house to settle in front of the fire with pipe and newspaper while I popped away to put the beloved G back in its place. The weather being so cold, I knew to use the lowest gear to ease the tractor back safely. All went well until time to put the clutch in neutral, and I couldn't do it!! It would not go into place! The determined low "POP, POPS" inexorably took me closer and closer to the side of the barn—and I panicked! I knew that I could not ride through the barn wall, killing myself and my unborn child. I leapfrogged off the back of that big tractor as it took down a huge corner post and about half of the north side of Daddy's barn. Believe it or not, I had enough mind left to run and catch this monster and stop it before it went on another rampage.

I tell our son Charles, who can be of a nervous and jumpy nature, that I marked him for life, almost taking him through the side of a barn on a run-away tractor. I learned, too, that if your child is well secured in its nesting place, there is no such thing as miscarriage.

From the perspective of my many years, I look back on this scene in wonder. My father certainly knew the finiteness of himself and his children, and he knew the hazards and fragility of life and how soon the "brief candle" could be extinguished; but he believed in me, didn't shelter me. The impact of this trust is a legacy for doing all things. That's a rare gift from a father to a child.

Mama and Daddy

My sassy, youthful pride came before the destruction of the barn; but like a good father, Daddy made every out for me: the cold weather, the new clutch, my inexperience at tractor driving. All was excused, all forgiven, and much thanksgiving went up for the deliverance of me and my unborn child from a G tractor gone wild. Jack came home and helped put the barn back together.

"I can do all things through Christ who strengthens me"—this passage from Paul's letters has been the bulwark of my years. The good father, the Heavenly Father, the Good Shepherd—all know our dichotomy of spirit—our humility and pride, our wisdom and foolishness, our love and hate, our honesty and dishonesty, our strength and weakness. We are saved from our pride and destruction. This love and trust of the Good Father is beyond all human understanding and the heart's knowing. It is forever.

Yea, though I drive through the side of a barn, surely goodness and mercy shall follow me all the days of my life and I will dwell in the barn indestructible forever.

46

My son, keep your father's commandments...Bind them about your heart always; tie them about your neck. When you walk, they will lead you; when you lie down, they will watch over you; and when you awake, they will talk with you.

Proverbs 6

My daddy would not have been a good Jewish patriarch. He said that they were so blind, so puffed up with themselves that they never recognized daughters, only sons. Daughters were little better than servants.

All the Proverbs were written to "my son," and Daddy questioned why the girls were never included. In fact, one of the Jewish Orthodox prayers thanks God for not being born a slave or a woman. After all these centuries, the Jewish female world is in rebellion with these new-millennium, liberated young girls demanding their bat mitzvahs—just as their brothers have had throughout their history—and that the Pentateuch and the Writings be rewritten to include them. Way to go, Rachel!!!

These Jewish girls would have liked my father's commandments and sayings. He insisted religion in general and churches in particular, would have died out long ago if the women's civilizing influences had not been there to check masculine ego. He approved the saying, "The hand that rocks the cradle is the hand that rules the world." The hand that rocks the cradle would never send its sons to war. He lamented how the masculine world, without any women in its policy making, was the warmongers, the tyrants who killed generation after generation of their sons. He insisted, if there were any fairness in the world's governments, the ladies would be given—maybe just five years—their chance to rule. He declared women had heard the great commandments, "Love your neighbor" and "Thou shalt not kill."

In the Jewish synagogues of old, the women were separated from the men by partitions and were never allowed to speak. "Ask your husband when you get home" was Paul's instruction for women. It was almost the same in my rural, totally-fundamental church. Daddy always said, "Our women are the wisest" and that was true. The best educated, the most articulate, the ones of deepest spirituality were the women.

He insisted they should be allowed to pray in public because he thought some of the men's prayers didn't get above their coattails. Women should be allowed to teach men, who as a whole were pretty stupid—and yes, even preach; and he didn't care what St. Paul or Moses said. I bound this liberation to my heart, and it works its wonders still.

"It doesn't cost anything to be kind." Now there's a saying of my father's that you can walk with. He was forever for the underdog and spent his days rendering whatever help he could to neighbors during the Great Depression years. His concern was for all men,

Mama and Daddy

both black and white, and these families, yet, honor his name. Two weeks ago last Sunday, I visited with a friend of those days who gave my father credit for helping him find means to finance a home. He had no use for arrogance or concern for blue blood or for the show of money. For him, I learned to love and accept, though imperfectly, and I yearn to do better with each passing year. His concern for all "sort and condition of men" still talks to me.

Daddy admonished us: "Don't be an old fogey." Now an old fogey was someone who never had a new idea, clung to the past and thought anything new the work of the Devil. My daddy was always on the cutting edge of the new. In his orchard, he grafted multiple varieties of fruit into one tree causing old fogies to declare him sinful, fooling around with the Lord's work. From the U.S. Extension Office, he came home with many innovations: building earthen storage bins, planting experimental canola seed, growing belladonna during World War II for medicinal purposes, gathering together scions of first-settlers' fruit trees, planting many exotic berries and grapes and building a proto-type rotary mower that he could never power; its sweep was too great.

My father's orchard was a work-of-art. "Do the best you can with what you've got." On the Sunday before the peaches were picked, he had what he called his reception when friends and neighbors were invited to look at and taste the work of his hands. He had given his orchard his heart and soul. A high school classmate insulted me by calling my father, "that peddler." He would not have cared one whit about this appellation, for that was part of his business, peddling his wares. The false pride was mine.

Children and dogs know who loves them. The dogs wagged, and Daddy pied-pipered several generations of children in our neighborhood who clustered around him for string tricks, riddles and all sorts of jokes. Old men now tell me of their love for him and of his legacy of laughter.

As he lay dying, I would ask him, "Daddy, how are you today?" And his answer was always the same. "I'm in great shape for the fix I'm in." He died with a beatific smile on his face.

So with my Jewish sisters, I include us in the Proverbs. *My daughter, keep your father's commandments; bind them about your heart, walk with them, sleep with them and talk with them. For length of days and years of abundant welfare will they give you.* On both sides of life everlasting, God keep all our fathers.

47

For some twenty years I was editor of The Trumpet. For the bleak month of January, I usually wrote something to warm the "cockles of our hearts." This story I have saved to protect my mother, who left us in 1987, in her 95th year.

> *Your mother shall be utterly confounded, and she who bore you shall be disgraced.*
>
> **Jeremiah 50**

My dear mother did aspire for her children and grandchildren to be ladies and gentlemen. With all her noble heart, how she tried. There was no strong language in our household, no double negatives, no improper use of knife and fork, no eating until all were served, no head-in-your-plate slurping, and no plate left awry. This was the table stuff. Social manners were another matter: hats off for men in the house, rising when company appeared, and "yes ma'ams" and "no sirs" all over the place. White gloves, trimmed hats, polished shoes, Saturday night scrubbings, and much starching and ironing were the norm. So went my mother who bore me. She gave me her best.

With the oncoming hippy generation, she was utterly confounded. Grandchildren were from another realm, one that so suddenly came upon her in her eighty plus years that she had no inkling about such ideas and values and practices. Poor gullible Granny. Living alone and getting crippled with arthritis, she would have accepted Lucifer himself to live with her in order to stay in her own home.

Mama and Daddy

Down from the big city came a teenage grandson who had gotten into the swing of the new age with all its pot-smoking and heavens-knows-what else. He came to Kirkwood, barefoot and long haired to be the succor of his grandmother. There is not time nor space to tell the tales of the clash of these two generations.

My dear mother did aspire for her children and grandchildren to be ladies and gentlemen.

With the grandson's coming, he needed wheels. "How dear," thought Granny. "He will need a truck next spring when he starts the garden." His garden had different ideas. In November, with Granny's money to back him up, my nephew traded with a used-car salesman and came triumphantly home with a shivering old truck, high off the ground and crowned with a rusty top and trimmed with fenders that had not fended well.

How this grandson hoisted my mother up into this chariot with all her aching bones I'll never know, but away they hurried to my

Mama and Daddy

house by way of Peachers Mill Road to show off their treasure. It was afternoon and they stayed for supper, which put them back on the road after dark. They chose to go back to Kirkwood by Kraft Street with its bustling traffic and alert traffic cops. Immediately they were pulled over.

In his exuberance to use their newly acquired wheels, my nephew casually dumped his license plate, his title, his driver's license on a shelf and took out with only one tail light.

The arresting officers threw the book at him, called a wrecker to come and impound the truck, all the while leaving my mother in the cab freezing in the cold November night. The officers did not see my mother. When the tow truck arrived and hitched to the prize, my nephew had to implore, "My grandmother is in that truck!"

Mama needs to tell her story at this point. "Well, I was frozen stiff, but these two lovely gentlemen lifted me out and put me in their patrol car. It was warm, but I did feel strange looking from the back seat cage with all the guns in front. To cap it all off, we stopped at every stop light in town, and I was in plain view."

The grandson was booked and put in the lock-up, but, of course, Mama was in whatever waiting room the jail had and was free to call. About 10:30, the phone rang. This little voice said, "You will have to come get me." Fearing a wreck, I said, "Mama, where are you?" Then in this big, booming voice—"I'm In the Jail." I fell back in the bed and laughed and laughed. Of all the incongruous places in the whole wide world for my Mama to be was in jail!

It was about eleven o'clock when I arrived to take my mother home. She, like a queen with her guards, was escorted down these long stairs by two most helpful and courteous patrol officers. She said she had never met nicer gentlemen. The jailers seeing my mother's classic demeanor, let her grandson out of his cell, instructing him to come back next day and pay his fines and ransom his truck. What a night to remember.

Mama and Daddy

Mama determined to be neither confounded nor disgraced. Her years and her struggles "to serve the Lord" had taught her to accept the human families' disgraces and confusions, especially this grandson's. Grandchildren were the crowning joy of her old age, and she kept their sins in her "forgiving and forgetting" section. She understood that we disgrace and confound ourselves. The mystery of the love of God, revealed to us in Christ, must become more clear with age, but I find myself still confounded and disgraced as I look inward. A slow learner is at hand, and I lean, not on two courteous police officers, but on the One who looks for lost sheep.

Mama and Daddy

PROPHESIES

48

And there followed him a great multitude of the people and of women who bewailed and lamented him. But Jesus turning to them said, "Daughters of Jerusalem do not weep for me but weep for yourselves and for your children. For behold the days are coming when they will say, 'Blessed are the barren and the wombs that never bore, and the breasts that never gave suck!' Then they will begin to say to the mountains, 'Fall on us; and to the hills, cover us.' For if they do this (crucify me) when the wood is green, what will happen when it is dry?"

Jesus on the way to the cross.   Luke 23

Daughters of Jerusalem, the wood is dry. For what shall we weep?

Weep for our unhearing ears that no longer hear the great commandments: Love God above all and your neighbors as yourselves. Forgetting the eternal infallibility of these two laws, we can only be doomed to weeping. The wood is dry and daily we are consumed.

Weep for us children of Hagar and Sarah that we live by the sword and die by the sword. Weep that the ages have taught us nothing.

Weep for our hardness of heart. "Love your enemies, feed your enemies, bless those who despitefully use you." Weep that we cannot turn the other cheek, but only the twist of the sword.

Weep for the cows of Bashan. With every sweet morsel, we gorge the temple of the spirit, our bodies, while half the world cries out for bread, the crumbs that fall from our table. Weep for swollen bellies and nothing to buy daily bread. Empty, we look away.

Prophesies

Weep for our worship of the golden calf. We shall build bigger barns to store our wealth and bigger bombs to bolster our Pride of Power. Our souls shall be required of us and innocent blood will call to God from the ground. Weep for His answer in terrible judgment. "His truth is marching on."

Weep, cry out for the mountains to fall on us, for the hills to cover us. Be thankful for no children when the wood is dry and exploding. Weep that we have made our own gods and have created our doom. Again, the snake has deceived us. Weep, ye Daughters of Jerusalem, ye Daughters of Baghdad, ye Daughters of the Potomac, and ye Daughters on the banks of the Xingu. "We have been weighed in the balance and found wanting."

Weep for us, the Church, the Body of Christ, His bride with the bloody hands. Weep ye, weep ye, and again I say, "Weep."

49

School days, school days, dear old Golden rule days; reading and writing and 'rithmetic, taught to the tune of a hickory stick...

A song from my childhood

My high school graduation class of 1940 had its sixtieth reunion on June 9th. My brother, who lives in Atlanta, was asked to be master of ceremonies, but he couldn't attend; therefore, I was slipped into this slot.

"Woodson, what shall I talk about? What shall I tell them?"

"Remind them of Miss Alzada Johnson's history class, especially current events day on Friday when you had to be up on what happened yesterday and last night. 'What did Hitler do?' I had no idea what Hitler did since I practiced football until almost sundown, hitch-hiked home down the Guthrie Highway to

Prophesies

Hampton Station Road, walked home two miles; and if Daddy hadn't milked the cows, I finished my day with the milk bucket.

We country boys were at a slight disadvantage. Our *Clarksville Leaf Chronicle* was mailed out on the rural route the day after it was published and we had no electricity—thus, no radio. Current events were a day late. When I was asked to answer, there I sat among much hand-waving from all the city boys; and I knew Miss Johnson labeled me "one of those dumb football players!"

Such were our school days in 1939.

In this year 2000, I have lived through this century of such swift and incomprehensible change that our school days of yesteryear seem fossilized, and the little children of this generation will lead us. From OK Tablets and No. 2 lead pencils, we see this generation instantly communicating with the whole world and reaching beyond; and we wonder what new work is being wrought before our wondering eyes. Is this another Gutenberg explosion of knowledge?

The 1940 Reunion Committee asked me to write a poem commemorating our sixty years as a class. I share this effort with you.

1940-2000 WHERE DID THE TIME GO?

Four score years, minus three or four
Find us breathless in millennium's door.
These fleeting days, gone by too fast
Hold us in wonder at all that's past…
Where did the time go?

In two-room rural academes
We found the beginning of our dreams,
Or in city hall of grander space
We began the passage of life's long race…
And we wonder—where did the time go?

Prophesies

We went to learning of high degree,
Or found our way in factory, or
On farm, or on war's woeful shore.
In store for our journey was more, much more...
Where did the time go?

The time has gone for work and play
For rearing a family, that's now away...
For disappointment, division, and disease...
For love and laughter and hearts at ease.
That's where the time did go.

The time is crowding; we're out of breath;
We face the final mystery—DEATH.
No medicine, no miracle, no device
Can keep us from that side of life...
That's where the time will go.

Years here have been prologue to life,
New life where joy is rife and right is right,
Where eyes unveiled can see most clear...
All that's past has brought us here...

And we count not time by years
For there is no night there.

RELATIVES & ACQUAINTANCES: SOME HERE AND SOME THERE

50

Parting is such sweet sorrow.

Romeo and Juliet

Our household has been bereft since our two grandsons, Patrick and Charles, returned to their home in Paris, France. On our Christian journey, God seems to break through our closed selves now and again and shows us a new dimension of His love for us. This love, which Paul says has been poured into our heart by the source of all love, came to me in our grandsons' "parting." Emily Dickinson said it succinctly—"parting is all we know of heaven and all we need of hell."

From the streets of Paris to Pollard Road is a broad jump. In Charles' eyes, the younger grandson, "Tennessee is the place to be because there's nothing to do in Paris." These are 12 and 14-year-old eyes that have the perspective of action, not beauty and culture. Their granddaddy has the viewpoint all boys need to learn how to work. "It keeps them out of trouble."

On their first day here, Daddy-Jack had a blackberry picking expedition planned, complete with high-top boots, sticks to part briars and scare snakes, chigger repelling potions at all exposed places, and small plastic buckets fitted with strings around their necks. With no complaining, they came in, sweaty and triumphant, with enough blackberries for two cobblers.

The next boy-discipline was fence mending. Jack says you have to have someone to "hold" to mend a fence. Away they went in the cool of the morning with their spools of barbed wire and wire-splicers to run the fence where the cattle crossed the shallows of the creek. Staple-holding got to be old hat, and Patrick got a good eye for the correct tautness of stretched wire. While out in the pasture they had to count the cattle, whose numbers were more than 100; and they learned to search the ravines and shady creek places for missing calves. They rejoiced over the lost steer and, no doubt, will hear the story of the one lost sheep with new ears.

Our boys were ready for motors. Their uncle, a genius of a fix-it, came home and it was lessons in oil-changing, tire-changing and general maintenance of the lawn mower. Patrick mowed the yard with a swaggering casualness as though he had been cutting yards for 50 years. Charles only had a turn in easy places. Before breakfast, you would hear the mower start up just for a quick ride-around and a good morning cleaning.

Charles Coffre, the red head, left, and Patrick Coffre, right.

The tractors had to be serviced—all the spark plugs, air conditioners, brakes and whatever. Two pairs of eager eyes and ears looked and listened. The final motor to be conquered was our old VW with a standard shift and a tricky clutch.

Granny got the VW detail. In the heat of the afternoon when we old folks should be cooling in the house, it was "Granny, let's go drive the car." With many a buck-jump and killed motor, Patrick at length got his long legs and the gears and clutch sorted out and was going up and down the drive quite well. Charles was another story. His legs were hardly long enough to reach the pedals, and he tended to watch his feet rather than the road, all the while calling himself "Jeff Gordon." One gate had a narrow escape and the bushes along our route were pruned a few times. Finally, he mastered the gear shifting and couldn't wait for fourth gear and SPEED. They were proud of themselves, feeling all grown up, and Granny felt, too—too hot and too old to coach such eagerness.

Tennessee's something-to-do went on and on. They steered the big tractor, they picked dozens and dozens of ears of corn for the freezer, they washed cars, they helped load cattle trucks headed for the feedlots and made all trips in the old truck to the Co-op and other farmer places.

After a month, parting was upon us. We hadn't talked about our separation and Charles, in particular, the night before their departure was for the first time quiet with a faraway look in his blue eyes. At bedtime, I went with him upstairs where he fell in my arms with such anguish as to break my heart. By the next afternoon when we went to the airport, I thought we had our composure together, but I was wrong. When their turn came to board the plane, we dissolved into a great turbulence of tears, Patrick on one side and Charles on the other as we clung together. There were grannies in the crowd. I saw tears and handkerchiefs as fellow travelers witnessed our parting.

As I mull and muse about this month of many graces, I feel a new depth of God's gift—that I can love this much and that my love is returned. There is no greater gift. Our kitchen table became an altar on which we shared blackberry pie and crusty cornbread, a sacrament of praise to a love so unending and sustaining that we know not its height nor depth; but we know it spans oceans and time and "that nothing in all creation can separate us from the love of God which is in Christ Jesus, our Lord."

51

In his funeral instructions, Cousin Billy Welker directed that I, his cousin Charlotte, should deliver his eulogy. This I did here at Trinity on August 6. Always John William Welker was known to me as, "Cousin Billy" and we were indeed kissing cousins à la française – a kiss on both cheeks and sometimes the third one if there arose some reason for celebration. Our cousin-relationship was special and with three kisses I send Cousin Billy on before me into that place of perfect love and peace.

> And I will show you a still more excellent way... For now, we see in a mirror dimly, but then face to face. Now I know in part, then I shall understand fully, even as I have been understood. So faith, hope, love abide, these three—but the greatest of these is love.
>
> **St. Paul I Corinthians 13**

Cousin Billy Welker in his life has shown me a more excellent way. We share a common heritage in Grandma Wickham who was his grandmother and my great grandmother. Coming from Virginia by way of North Carolina and down the rivers of Tennessee, our pioneer forebears brought with them a hope for excellence that has come to fruition in one of their sons—John William Welker.

Grandma Wickham put such emphasis on education that she sold part of her land grant at Palmyra to send two of her ten children to school—Dr. John Wickham and my maternal grandmother, Belle Wickham. Ever before Grandma was the great legacy of education. I owe personally Cousin Billy's family a debt of gratitude. When my mother was eight years old, she and her two sisters were orphans and lived by the charity of relatives. With great faith and hope, Grandma Wickham sent them to her daughter Emma—Billy Welker's mother—who welcomed them into her already big family and saw to their education at the Stewart County Academy at Erin. When my mother was eighteen, she took the examination for teaching in the public schools of this county and began her career at Jordan Springs' one room school. Thanks to the love and care of

Relatives & Acquaintances

Billy's mother, I was never allowed to use double negatives, incorrect pronouns, not to mention butchered past participles. Even our grammar had been shown a **still** more excellent way.

Billy's big family of ten children moved from Erin to Clarksville where Aunt Emma, taking up Grandma's banner, had faith and hope for the education of her two youngest children—John and Robert—her students, who, to quote Tennyson, "would follow knowledge like a sinking star." Early in high school, Cousin Billy came under the inspiration of our own Dorothy Ann Russo in her French class. The course of his star was set by her teaching, and he followed its path to the absolute zenith of his chosen profession—that of French professor.

At Austin Peay State University he held this chair for many years. I personally can attest to his excellence as a teacher, even though he could never teach my southern accent not to corrupt the French language. He received his Bachelor's degree from Austin Peay State University and did graduate work at Middlebury College in Vermont and at Vanderbilt University.

His highest honor, however, was conferred on John William Welker by the French Government. He received the most coveted of all French honors—The Legion of Honor in the field of Arts and Letters. He had so promoted French culture through his teaching, through his travels and his discourses with French intellectuals, and with the exchange programs of French students that the French nation chose to honor him with its highest accolades. I was there when the Consul came from the French consulate in New Orleans to bestow the medal and ribbons on this adopted son. We, Grandma Wickham, Aunt Emma, and I, cousin Charlotte, rejoice that our hopes have been so fulfilled in this, our own blood son.

The "more excellent way" somehow sums up John Welker's life. He was a searcher, not only for knowledge, but for excellence. In all areas of his life—in his home, in his dress, in his speech, in his yard, in his teaching, in his entertaining—he gave his utmost efforts. How many times he and Marcelite had us in their home where we were served in an elegant setting of silver and linen and china with the choicest of cheeses and wine. We were made to feel special and cherished. He had no peer as a host. Certainly one of his most excellent choices was Marcelite who complemented him with every good and perfect gift. Not only did he choose one of the best English teachers in Clarksville, but certainly he chose one of the finest cooks.

John Welker was a questioner, one who did not hanker for pat answers or easy answers. His questions of life and death and the fabric of our existence were hard ones that have been wrestled with since man became a cognizant being. His faith was a questioning faith, one seen through a mirror dimly, which, in the long run, is the only honest faith. As he drew nearer to the end of his life, he seemed to grasp more fully a dimension beyond the self, a hope in the face of the great mystery of Death. And I felt his love become more complete as he dismissed the struggles of his life here and yielded himself to "the more excellent way."

As we who are left here in our grief seek hope and faith, we again hear St. Paul as he assures us of this excellent way, one that cannot be taken from us.

> *For I am sure that neither death, nor life, nor angels, nor principalities, nor things present, nor things to come, nor powers, nor height, nor depth, nor anything in all creation will be able to separate us from the love of God in Christ Jesus our Lord.*
>
> **Romans 8**

52

Marriage: A lifetime sentence with no time off for good behavior.

A family saying

Today, May 15, is our fifty-sixth wedding anniversary. Our romantic greetings to each other on this celebratory morning were these: "Fifty-six years is too long to be married to any old man," and my husband's reply, quoting an aged friend, "I'm going to get me a young wife. I had rather smell perfume than liniment."

Having lived this long together without murder or blood-letting or walking out, we give thanks that we are left with a sense of humor and a deep sense of wonderment at the pleasure, the pain, the fulfilled dreams, and the greatest gift of all—the creative miracle of our three children. What a struggle! What a life! And I wouldn't have missed any of it.

During WW II, romance often was a dicey and hurried proposition. Ft. Campbell cleaned out Clarksville of all old maids and even one lonely maiden, wheelchair bound. Men were about twenty to one and if a girl were willing, choices abounded. There were good marriages and bad ones, too-soon-widowed ones, and, yes, polygamous ones with every sort of

Jack, the boy next door, was away at sea all during the war.

deception that young men, who thought they might not come back, could make into a fast line. War makes hormones flow fast and juggles judgment. Uniforms and bars and stripes and service medals make a girl's patriotic blood stand at attention and a non-pedigreed "dog face" look good. Such are the annals of war and the marriages thereof.

I was caught in this dizzying era. Jack, the boy next door, was away at sea all during the war, riding high octane gasoline across the North Atlantic to fuel Mars' fighting machines. You did not survive a torpedoed tanker. He was at home for short furloughs and down to the sea again. Once, at home he told me if I ever wanted to get married to let him know, and that's what I did. Here was a man I knew would tell the truth and would stand fast when the going got tough. Too, he was my ticket to a new world, away from kith and kin and Kirkwood, away from bucolic innocence, into the real world.

We had a small window of days to get married, less than a week.

We had a small window of days to get married, less than a week. Not counting my engagement ring, my wedding may have cost a hundred dollars. I still give thanks to my mother-in-law who recruited the Reverend J. Earl Gilbreath, the priest at Trinity, to perform the ceremony in my Baptist family's living room. Amid many lamentations of "marry in haste; regret at leisure," distress at whiskey-drinking Episcopalians and gambling tendencies in the Marshall clan, the knot was tied. On our side was my daddy; he knew a good man when he saw one.

So away I went to a new world—to New York on an airplane and then to Montreal; and afterwards, following my seafaring husband, to most ports on the East and West Coasts and the Gulf of Mexico. After the war was over, I flew to Europe and sailed my then ship's-captain husband's ship back across the North Atlantic to Philadelphia. Kirkwood was never the same again. I had seen Paris, but my dirt-between-the-toes-sailor managed to keep me down on the farm.

Let's be honest. We marry for many reasons. There is steamy passion. This wasn't for me because my mother had instilled in me that if I as much as looked cross-eyed at a man I would be pregnant. I won't be rewarded for being good; I was too afraid not to be. For me there was a mixture of curiosity, of hope, of beginning, of daring to break old fears, to find someone to share my dreams of a home and children, and someone to lean on as a friend, and, yes, in the process be my lover and the father of my children. True passion is the flowering of lives given away to each other.

After these fifty-six years, for me love and respect have become synonymous. The more I respect my husband the more I love him. Even through some dark days of disagreement and opposing ideals, I knew basically the bare-bones integrity of this man and that ultimately he would be found on the side of what was right and true. Struggling to keep a marriage together is one of life's most difficult tasks, and we had absolutely no training for being good wives and husbands. It was trial and error, mostly error, and I have no judgment for those who abandon the whole project and then try the blessed institution again—and maybe again…and again.

Yes, and again we return to the gospel—the good news, even for our earthly marriages. It has been said that a good relationship is a 50-50 proposition, meeting halfway. That won't do it. It must be a willing 100 percent of giving to the other, just as God does not meet us halfway, but is eternally there always ready to take us back, to forgive us, show us the way through our messes, and teach us, through our pain, that we are beloved sons and daughters, children of his eternal passion.

To you starry-eyed June brides and expectant grooms, you old married folk, you disillusioned young married folk, or divorced folk, and all folk living in varied relationships, let us hear anew these words—"Little children let us love one another, for love is of God and God is Love."

53

Fish and visitors smell in three days.

Benjamin Franklin

When I was a child, July was the month of visitors. Kirkwood was the halfway point between Florida and Ohio, and we got two sets of relatives, coming and going. A week's rest was needed after each leg of this migration since the open-air touring cars had broiled its occupants to well-done, requiring much fanning and rocking on our front porch. With golf bags, soured suitcases, a love-sick adolescent, a stone-deaf aunt, a Jehovah's Witness with many pamphlets, and a harmonica player—here they came, all with voracious appetites.

These were Daddy's relatives, which did not endear them to Mama, either blood-wise or religious-wise, her being of the Baptist persuasion. With the sun at its apogee, she had to extend her backside to the sun god to appease the appetites of these butterbean-starved relations. Butterbeans flourish on the hottest days and yield their beans reluctantly, especially in great volumes that ruin your thumbnails. Added to this was chicken-plucking, tomato gathering, corn shucking, and all the duties of a Southern kitchen. One year to further complicate this visit, the two-week revival meeting was going on at Kirkwood Baptist Church. We had going at the same time hellfire, damnation, and a complete exegesis of the Book of Revelation. This cross-current of theology was almost too much for our household.

Some of the Jehovah's witness-converts would go to the Baptist revival for ammunition against such free offers of salvation. The Revelation stated simply that there were to be one-hundred-and-forty-four thousand sealed to be saved and these slots were, no doubt, for Jehovah's Witnesses. Sitting at the kitchen table by a dim kerosene lamp, one uncle would write way into the wee hours explaining, "I am writing an account of the final days to God's woman." This was the time when the Whore of Babylon would be ousted, she who was "drunk with the blood of the saints and blood of the martyrs of Jesus."

Mama finally got fed up, gathered us children together, and went to spend the day with Miss Julia. On Mama's table there was no hot cornbread, no chicken, no butterbeans, no nothing; and we stayed until meeting time that night. When we got home, they were gone, and there had been no rapture, no rising to meet Jehovah in the air.

Poor Daddy! He tried to love these aunts and cousins but vowed religion had "kinked their brains."

"What fools these mortals be." That includes all of us. In trying to find our meaning of God, the riddle of our existence, a morality to root ourselves to this puzzling planet, we have defined our God in all generations to fulfill our needs and to nail down our corner on the Truth. All our philosophies render God even more mysterious, more beyond knowing, and we long to be those little children who accept the Kingdom of God without question.

The Jew's wrote their history of Jehovah as a fierce warrior who gave them the Promised Land. Moses continued the tradition of the fierce God who burned the Law in stone and punished all who fell short of the Law. But by Jesus' time, this God and the Law were called into question by the Father of the Prodigal Son, a most loving and forgiving God, one who sent us an example of himself.

Relatives & Acquaintances

Cousin Ed found his Truth in the Second Coming, in his knowing exactly what the Book of Revelation meant. Our Baptist revival preacher found his Truth in hellfire and damnation and went back to the fierce God of the Jews.

Jesus said there were only two laws and both were alike: Love God first and your neighbor as yourself. On this hangs our reason for being. Creative love is the most powerful force in all creation—yes, this is God. "God is love." Self love and pride destroy. Love for God and neighbors will restore all things: Israel and Palestine; our beloved country and Iraq; even summer visitors and the Revelation of John. If only through the ages, we had heard this eternal <u>Truth</u>. Personally and nationally, may we hear the Law of Love anew.

54

Some of us call it autumn
And others call it God.

W.H. Carruth

The world is ablaze with autumn. Awestruck, I stand like a prism—infusing all these colors into my remembrance—against the bare days of winter. Who can know the author of this unutterable beauty? Who can paint the whole creation? Until we no longer see through the "glass darkly", we shall call his name—God.

Cousin Bedford Forrest Blackwell had God and his creation literally explicated. Some six thousand years ago, God spoke all—everything—into being in six days, again, at one speaking, the layers that anthropologist dig for dating, just to confound the upstart scientist. Referring to the Book of Revelations, he knew the actual time of the last dispensation when he and the elect would be taken up in the rapture. He lived in a barren world, looking only for glory in the world to come, unaware of the glory of the here and now.

At the opposing pole, stood my cousin, Edwin Winn, from California. The creation story was all myth, an oral tradition handed down through the ages, that was finally recorded by the Jewish nation. Their god was a God of blood and wrath that no one should ever follow. Charles Darwin had it right. We are an evolved species, a notch ahead of apes, not a little lower than angels. The plants have risen from lower forms until we now have the deciduous trees that show color in the fall and then lose their leaves. He was all science and no sentiment—cold facts that obliterated beauty and mystery. These must be some country beyond my cousins, some place where autumn is God.

This morning as I walked in these days of crown jewels and diadems, I knew both creation and evolution. From some mystery beyond all knowing, I was created a cognitive being with a heart that sustains this creation. Through the years this heart has evolved from one innocent and unknowing, to one youthful and rebellious, to one finally drawn out of itself toward a creative flame that has warmed me into a reflection of a mighty radiance. This is a glow, a gift of Grace.

As October pales into November and into our season of Thanksgiving, let us give praise to a creation that calls us out, not to comprehend, but to behold. Let cousins be confounded. Let faith be confirmed that all are held in arms beyond all knowledge. Let us bask in the presence of a glory that warms our hearts and affirms that we are loved through all our sorrow, folly, and confusion. As surely as autumn comes, God is here.

55

Tobacco is a dirty weed. I like it.
It satisfies no normal need. I like it.
It makes you thin, it makes you lean,
It takes the hair right off your bean.
It's the worst darn stuff I've ever seen.
I like it.

Graham Lee Hemminger: Tobacco

It's January, Dear Reader, and you know our dead-of-winter tradition for *Mullings and Musings*. It has us waxing merry lest January days, depressingly cold and short of sun, creep into our very bloodstreams. The medicine of the merry heart is our prescription three times a day and with tea. To start our blood coursing in the right direction, I now administer an elixir, laced with tobacco, and coupled with an account of sweet motherly revenge. As background I refer you to page 21 in the compilation of *Mullings and Musings, volume 1*.

Here is more background: my husband was a sailor in the Merchant Fleet during World War II and for some years after 1945. When he came home from sailing this alien milieu, away from the farm, he came laden with chocolates and many cartons of cigarettes from the ship's "slop chest." Being most inexpensive and ubiquitous at this point in our nation's history, these cigarettes were dispensed generously to friends and relatives, particularly to my father-in-law, Jim P. Marshall. My husband smoked an occasional cigar or pipe, but never cigarettes.

Upon one homecoming, our five-year-old son—the devious one who tricked his mother with the "hot" vacuum cleaner episode—came upon his father unpacking his gifts and calmly announced, while eating a mouthful of chocolates, that he wanted to learn to smoke. No one paid this deliberate and determined child any attention; and when we noticed him again he was sitting on the front porch, cross-legged and chocolate smeared, smoking one cigarette off another. A visiting nephew caught this smoke-out

Relatives & Acquaintances

snapshot for posterity. To my knowledge, these are the only cigarettes that our son has ever smoked.

Now to relate sweet payback time: After the vacuum cleaner foolishness and with all the merry genes of my brother and this son so satiated, I had to do something. December 2nd is this son's birthday. So what does Mama do? She sends their son's smoking photo to the Columbus, Georgia, *Ledger-Enquirer* for their personal page, which had the title *Happy Ads*. There for all the Columbus world to see was a picture of this five-year-old, neglected, delinquent, child smoking away on a cigarette. Here's the *Happy Ad*:

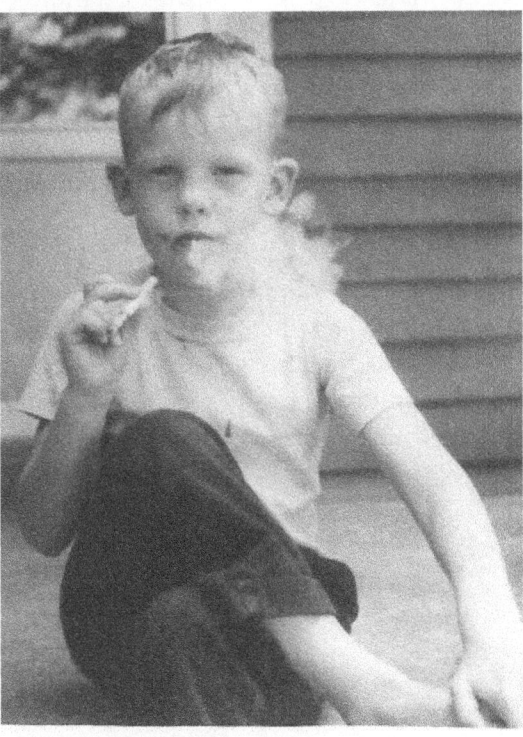

Happy Birthday
Woodson Polk Marshall
December 2, 1958

We had our doubts about you at age five. Now you control the entire Southeastern market on "hot" vacuum cleaners. We're so proud!
Love, Mama.

To make this get-even, even sweeter, our son, who arises early, cooks breakfast and reads the paper, saw his picture before he went to work. He said he wondered at first glance —"What poor, white-trash child is that?" Then after a closer look, "Hey, that's me!"

All day long, up and down the street, cars came to a sudden stop for his friends to laugh; and at work his picture was posted in all areas. "Did your mama really let you smoke?" and he assured them that I did since we all chewed and smoked and made our living from tobacco. To be honest, the "dirty weed" paid many of our bills. "I like it."

I'm sure my mother would not approve of this recounting because she was great on family *pride*. But is not *pride* oftentimes the problem? Somehow this tale is a study into our humanity, into our need to laugh in the face of all that pretends and keeps us uptight about our vision of the "perfect" family and the "perfect" self. When we accept that there is absolutely no possibility for perfection in any area, that's when we give up and laugh at dirty faces and the spontaneity of children. Moreover, there is trust implicit in this tale. My son and I have a relationship of mutual vulnerability, one that requires no eggshell walking.

Let us welcome any joy, any comic relief that gives us respite from our daily sorrows and the shadows of death. As God asked Job, "Where were you when the morning stars sang together and all the sons of God shouted for joy?"

I wish I had been there when the morning stars sang together, and I surely want to be here—right now—when the sons of God shout for joy. For the New Year let us hold fast to all the funny bone places and, in turn, surrender to a strength not ours at our weeping places. For "weeping may endure for a night, but joy cometh in the morning." "I like it."

Happy New Year! I love you all, COM

56

Home is Where the Heart Is

After World War II, my favorite cousin was buried in Philadelphia. He was a red-haired Adonis, his crisp curls atop a broad brow with eyes shining brown, all speckled with darker flakes. His infant beauty had been legendary, and he carried these winsome characteristics to his six feet and more and kept all us younger cousins charmed with his teasing good humor and his condescension to play with us. He was our hero.

The war came. He was whisked away to sea during the navy's darkest days, riding the North Atlantic into the maelstrom of German submarines, where he experienced "abandon ship" and the gunning down of his shipmates. I don't know the naval term for "shell shock," but my cousin never could rid himself of the terrible sights and sounds of his mates in their death agonies; and he wondered why he was spared.

To add a bitter layer to this sad sea story, my cousin was assigned new duty in the medical division of the navy and was trained as a pharmacist-mate, where he became acquainted with all medications. He slipped himself relief from his nightmares, and in the process became addicted to whatever opiate he had chosen. To make this very long story short, he died from this addiction, leaving a wife and a son who was a mirror-image of his father.

How fate or predestination or God's will finds us in certain places, I do not know. My husband and I were living in Baltimore at the time of my kinsman's death, and his sister came to us so we could be at her brother's funeral in Philadelphia the next day. The parents were too shocked and bereft to come.

What a day this funeral day was. If Dickens could have described this dark, misty day, it would have served his novel well; or if the moors of *Wuthering Heights* had suddenly come to us, that would be the setting. As we puzzled our way from Baltimore to

Philadelphia, the sky wept for us. Losing his way, my husband hailed a cab in Philadelphia, stuffed my cousin and me in, and gave the driver the address of the funeral home, leaving my husband to find his way there as best he could. We were late and the service was held for our arrival.

As we came into this strange hall, who was standing there to meet us but our Uncle McBryde Austin from the sandy plains of North Carolina! What a comfort that this tired old uncle came to support us. He was that kind; he knew we needed him.

This service for the dead was totally foreign to our Baptist and Presbyterian ways. My cousin had married an old-world Catholic; and her church's funeral customs seemed ghoulish to us, especially when we were invited to come forward and kiss the corpse goodbye. We were frozen in our seats; and I'm sure the priest and all the widow's family saw us as pagans. This remembrance seems like a bad dream, something that you store in your memory's attic and don't allow out. The pain is too sharp.

After the service was over and my husband had gotten to the address, Uncle Mac took us to a restaurant for supper. There, this good and noble Scotsman revealed to us a new dimension of life. His Presbyterianism served him well.

Suddenly he said, "You girls need a little whiskey," and with that he ordered bourbon, gave each of us a tablespoonful, and downed the rest himself. He addressed all of us nieces with a very long and southern "honey." So he begin—"Honey, I've begun to see death as going home. If it weren't for Ada and the girls, I'd be ready." His favorite sister, Hallie, had died during the flu epidemic of World War I; his brother, Hector, had died as a very young man; and he lost his only son when he was a child. He named the aunts, parents, and other relatives who were gone. "I have more on the other side than I have here, and I'm ready to go when I'm called home." He didn't live long after our last supper.

Now, as I approach an age greater than Uncle Mac's at the time of his death, I am beginning to feel the pull and the promise of the other side of life; however, I have not been separated on this side so severely as some I know—some who have lost all, like Job. And we look at them, wordless, and wonder—"how, dear God, how do they survive? Why, dear God, why are they called to this level of sacrifice?"

I am confused in a cloud of mystery at the disappointments of life, the seemingly unfairness of life, the total uncertainty of life, and the final sufferings of life. If it were not for the example our friend and savior, Jesus Christ, who has gone before us in all the trials and sufferings of our days here, we would be without hope. He knew it all. He was despised and disappointed, unfairness was his lot on all scores, his life was in an uncertain balance at all times; and his final suffering was nails in his hands and feet. He has shown us the way—with unconditional love and without bitterness—all the way to the other side of life. Through our fears and tears let us hear these comfortable words:

> *In my Father's house are many mansions; if it were not so, I would have told you. I go to prepare a place for you...that where I am, there ye may be also.*
>
> *John 14   KJV*

57

As recorded in *The Leaf Chronicle*: Primitive artist Enoch James Wickham, has brought fame to our family—a $40,000 grant to restore his legacy of primitive art! What relative would believe this? As Christ said, "A prophet is not without honor save in his own country."

Relatives & Acquaintances

Joseph clad in overalls with a real carpenter's pencil in his bib.

Uncle Tanner Wickham was a patriot. He celebrated with loud sounding trumpets, blasts of firearms, drops from heaven, eloquent orations, and monuments to illustrious soldiers, statesmen, and countrymen—some quick, some dead. He immortalized these in concrete and steel and was the artist who was determined to leave behind him a historic record of great men and events.

Uncle Tanner was the last of Grandma Wickham's ten children. Some of the relatives determined that Tanner had a "different streak" and some declared him "no count and lazy" because of his neglecting his family, dreaming up unrealistic schemes, and finally settling himself into full time dedication to the arts—this being the building of massive statue on the Canaan Road just out from Palmyra.

His first effort in concrete, his chosen medium, was the Virgin Mary. How Mary and Joseph came into Uncle Tanner's life down in his hills and hollows is somewhat of a mystery, but he had an experience, an epiphany, that caused him to turn a wash pot upside down, plaster it with concrete, and bring the Virgin and child forth for Palmyra's veneration. Joseph followed, clad in overalls, with a real carpenter's pencil in his bib. Tanner never hesitated to use real objects to vivify his statues. Andrew Jackson's horse had horseshoes, saddle, and bridle, all nicely coordinated with the right paint for dappling and highlighting.

Relatives & Acquaintances

Uncle Tanner's two most ambitious works were his equestrian statue of Andrew Jackson and his bull-riding, self-statue, each made from tons of concrete, steel rods, rolls of chicken wire, several sizes of stove pipes for molds, and some electrifying effect for the bull. Uncle Tanner made a trip to Nashville to study the statue of Andrew Jackson at the Capitol and determined to make the piece as near a replica in size as possible. It was—and still is—impressive. Now the bull-riding-Tanner-Wickham was his masterpiece. He featured himself astride this massive bull with the bull's tail drawn up over his shoulder as he caught the bull in a high-rodeo buck. On the base were inscribed these words, "Tanner Wickham gone to the wild and woolly west. Remember me, boys, when I'm gone."

Uncle Tanner was patriotic and political and the twain did meet. After World War II and his having lost a son in the war, he erected a monument to the young men from the Palmyra-Shiloh area who didn't come home. The Fort Campbell band came for the dedication along with a firing squad for salutes, and it all wound up with a big-brass speech and a parachute drop. Always political candidates were invited to these occasions and responded to the invitations from as far away as Washington, D.C.

A day to remember was Estes Kefauver Day. All the hopeful candidates from the local constable to the vice-presidential candidate were there. Babies and barbecue were in abundance and speeches orated from Uncle Tanner's newly-erected platform were the order of the day. Estes and other dignitaries rowed themselves up on this outdoor dais, constructed mostly from green sassafras saplings. In the course of one candidate's appeal, a wasp's nest was disturbed, causing hat-slapping panic and flamenco dancing. The structural engineering of the platform was put to the test and was found wanting. With teetering and

Uncle Tanner's gentle little sheep.

tottering and leaning, the platform at length collapsed, causing the candidates to disentangle their dignity from this sassafras morass.

In the course of his artistic life, Uncle Tanner immortalized Alvin York; John Kennedy; his brother, Dr. John Wickham; all the doctors from his area; Judge Pete Hudson of Clarksville; Patrick Henry; the early settlers of this county; and other unsung heroes. His concrete statue park became known as Wickham's Park. Across the road was his religious life expressed in many figures: Joseph and Mary, shepherds and angels, gentle little sheep, and kneeling children. His favorite hound dogs were sleeping at the arched entrance to this shrine, which included the largest sundial in the world. Uncle Tanner checked *Guinness Book of Records* and made his sundial two feet larger in diameter. When the sun was shining, the correct time was there.

Laugh if you like at Uncle Tanner. That's what his community did. Since his death vandals have decapitated Andrew Jackson, torn the horns off the bull and emasculated him, broken his Liberty Bell, and generally defaced his work. Weeds and vines have overgrown the sundial and angels, but if you search you can still find some vestiges of these. APSU did have his hound dogs in the theater building, and some of his statues made the World's Fair in Knoxville. There was honor away from home.

God in his wisdom has made each of us special, each with his rare gifts. Some of us never let ours awake, and we are bitter and find fault with our brothers' and sisters' expressions of creativity. Uncle Tanner never considered any of these judgments. He set his goal to create an historical record of his beloved country. Even though time and ignorance have marred his statues, his spirit and determination live on. May we on this 4th of July, 1998, say with Uncle Tanner and Sir Walter Scott—"This is my own, my native land!"

58

Human history becomes more and more a race between education and catastrophe.

H. G. Wells

Grandma Wickham believed in education. It was the open door to an ever expanding world—new ideas, new philosophies, all exploration in an increasing study of the human body, and above all, "to follow knowledge like a sinking star." She was a widow with ten children and she chose two of them to educate, they being, in her estimation, the two brightest of the ten.

In part, this story is told by my mother, who at eight years of age, was sent to Grandma's, along with three siblings, to live as best they could. Her father was killed in a railroading accident and her mother was sent away (hush! hush!) to Murfreesboro to an insane asylum where she lived for many years.

But back to Grandma and her decision. She found John Wickham and Belle Wickham her best candidates for higher learning. After much soul-searching, she chose John because he always had his nose in a book, didn't follow his brothers in their merry-making and moonshine, and had no interest in their quest for the loose girls and their "tumble in the hay." All this was beyond him. As to the girls, Belle was chosen hands down. She was a dreamer. She lost herself in the dishpan, trying to remember the lines of some poet, and spent the whole afternoon with one set of dishes. She dreamed of being a teacher, long before she met Rogers Livingston, and living out of the hollow at Palmyra, some romantic place, somewhere away from her present circumstances. Those were her dreams.

Being a widow, without consultation with a husband, she resolved to sell off two thousand acres of her land grant to finance this determination. Dr. John William Wickham was one of the first graduates of Vanderbilt Medical School, and he chose to come home to Palmyra to tend to the needs of a doctorless community. From my mother's testimony, there were hopeless cases bought to him—prostate cancer and colon cancer—and he had to send them away. There was no hope, no cure at that time.

But there were legions of cases he could cure. There was typhoid fever, malaria, intestinal ailments, childbirth problems, and on and on went the newest knowledge that Vanderbilt had to offer. Mama next reported on Belle. She was enrolled in some school for girls in Nashville, but I suspect that Rogers Livingston got her attention and she was married before she was twenty. She had four stair-step children, one of them my mother. The bomb fell when their "Poppa" was killed and the four children and mother had to go back to Grandma's.

All this was too much for Belle and she cracked, became depressed and violent, and after much family consideration, it was deemed best that she be sent away. This was before any medication for depression and when a family member was sent away there was no coming back, a life time sentence. Quite by accident, I learned of this when I was a grown woman, and it cleared up many mysteries about my mother's childhood.

For many years, John Wickham was the family doctor for his community. He was venerated for his diagnoses and his radical cures concerning typhoid fever. He had learned at Vanderbilt not to starve his patients but to feed them, to give them much to drink rather than no fluids. But all was not well with him.

Uncle John had one sickly daughter. Pearl died when she was six years old, leaving him and his wife bereft of their one child. They lost themselves in politics, in community health, in caring for their old mother's land grant. The land grant, based on service in the Revolution, was given to one of the Wickhams whose name I do not know. When the family crossed the mountains into Tennessee, they were given some 6000 acres of hills and hollows around Palmyra. This land grant was mostly timber land with creek bottoms along the way and easily claimed by other people looking for a home.

Relatives & Acquaintances

Charlie Baggett was one of the suspects, according to Uncle Tanner's daughter, who had a fertile imagination. She said Dr. Wickham was going into town to check on his grant and the surveyor's records. "Not so," said a niece of Uncle John's who wrote a detailed account of the murder. Here are her remembrances:

"Dr. Wickham was shot by Charles Baggett as he was getting on the train to go to Clarksville. Mortally wounded, he was taken by the train he was boarding to Nashville General Hospital, where he died. Before 8 o'clock the morning of the shooting, Dr. Wickham received a note written by Charles Baggett's housekeeper as Charles could not read or write. It concerned a log wagon of which each had agreed to pay half. Dr. Wickham had paid his half, but Charley had defaulted on his. In anger, Dr. Wickham rode his horse to where Charles was staying with his housekeeper, a half mile away. They had an argument and Dr. Wickham left, very angry.

Charley Baggett shot Dr. Wickham twice and, as he was on the ground, shot him a third time. He told Dr. Wickham he was his best friend, but that Dr. Wickham had made him do it. A jury trial held two years later resulted in a hung jury, with eight for acquittal and four for conviction on murder charges. Charley Baggett died before a second trial could be held. The train still passes the spot where Dr. Wickham was shot, but no sign remains of the station or the settlement of Hackberry."

The sad tale was settled out of court by a gathering of local farmers and some local officials. They didn't want to make matters worse. To the bitter end, Uncle Tanner's daughter said it was more a killing over land than anything else, but remember, she had a one-sided recollection.

Back in those days it was a common occurrence for men to settle their grievances with a gun. Uncle John was a victim of such justice. Whether he was guilty or not, now, so long ago, and seen through the eyes of a child—my mother's—the facts are indeed dim. He was a hero to an orphan child, and she, like all else, kept these things in her heart.

59

...And God said to them, be fruitful and multiply and fill the earth and subdue it and have dominion over everything that moves upon the earth.

Genesis 1

My mother-in-law took the Lord God literally. She was fruitful and multiplied, but above all, she had dominion over and subdued every living thing that moved upon the earth of Rossview and greater Montgomery County. This included all animate flesh, its occasions and organizations: her children, in-laws, grandchildren, neighbors, household pests, the family cat, the chicken house, all birthdays, anniversaries, Mother's Day, Father's Day, all holidays, Country Women's Club, Kirkwood Home Demonstration Club, Kirkwood Community Club, County Women of the World, Farm Bureau, Rossview Ladies Aid, PTA, County Fair, various card societies, all drives (heart, kidney, and rheumatism), all annual picnics and bazaars, all quilt-chance raffles, plus the spiritual directorship of the straying communicants of Grace Chapel, Rossview. Each of us living things—be we biped, quadruped, domestic, civic, churched or unchurched—was expected to fill its place in creation as it was ordained by this ninety pound Bishop of Rossview.

The Bishop, fondly known to us as Mary-Jim, had an urgency in her nature, a souped-up psyche set on fast forward that subdued all around her. If she were not president or otherwise organizer of the above mentioned, she set up a puppet regime which she directed with an iron determination that somehow seemed her right. She had been endowed with a hysterical spontaneity for immediate problem solving. With whoops of laughter she, and only she, knew how to get jobs done, and any anarchy was quickly subdued. We knew dominion when we saw it—and that included the family cat and me. We were in attendance to the Bishop on *Roll Day*.

Now Roll Day was the baking and freezing of dozens and dozens of rolls for all organizations and celebrations. Had the entire complement of Ft. Campbell suddenly bivouacked on her front lawn she could have furnished every man in his regiment a half-dozen hot, buttered rolls within the hour. On Roll Day, her staccato heels punished the linoleum and rattled the teacups—back and forth from the flour bin to kneading board to stove to cooling boards. Kitty and I were standing by to see how we fitted into this flurry of flour.

He meowed around our legs, tickled us with his twining tail, and enjoyed the warmth of the kitchen while I offered what paltry assistance I could to one so intently organizing the flour and pans. Now Mary-Jim believed in flour-not some little five-pound throwaway sack you could hold in the palm of your hand, but a great sack of D&F which was put in a cavernous bin in a venerable kitchen cabinet with a bread-kneading place on top. This bin had a weight in the bottom and you pulled it out and it flopped back in again, suggesting it might bite your arm off if you weren't careful. With this copious supply of flour on hand, she was ready to begin.

Mary-Jim put on her apron, got out her biggest mixing bowl, found the sifter with the reel inside, got out a great stack of pans, kicked the cat out of the way, pulled open the flour bin, peered in among the rolling pins and the biscuit cutters, gathered her skirt around her in a mighty flamenco, and let out a S C R E A M that made the original hole in the ozone. A mouse was in the flour! Creation was in chaos! Without missing a step, the Bishop assigned Kitty to his rightful place in the hierarchy of the universe, pulled out the bin, dropped him, and let it fly shut. There was a muffled thumping and bumping inside, and when to Mary-Jim's satisfaction enough time had elapsed for this subduing, she released her skirt, pulled open the bin, and there, wild-eyed and changed from gray to white, was Kitty with the poor squeaking, floured mouse in his jaws. Mary-Jim rejoiced in this triumph and deposited both outside the back door for Kitty to do his final dominion. Order had been restored in creation.

What moral can I muster from the late Bishop of Rossview? It must belong to the mighty bishops of this world. They would do well to attend: Roll Day is at hand. You have been imbued with power. Use it. Don't pussyfoot around. Throw your kitty in the flour bin lest the master of the house find you not using what you have. "That which you have may be taken away!"

60

Let not a widow be taken into your number under three score years old, having been the wife of one husband . . . but the younger widows refuse, for when they have begun to wax wanton against Christ, they will marry.

1 Timothy

June is the month for weddings. My grandmother had many a tale to tell of her romances, of widowhood, of slanderous accusations against her during this state, and of her nose-thumbing at St. Paul's rules for the deportment of widows. Romance waxed her wanton twice after having been a "true" widow at twenty.

Grandmother's first husband, my father's father, died when Daddy was two. Greene Oliver had come riding into Rudolphtown, down from Louisville, looking for a farm and a good wife. Mattie Winn caught his eye even though she had been known to do some two-stepping behind Little Hope Baptist Church. But true love would win out, and my grandfather married Mattie when she was eighteen.

After his death, Grandmother recalled her desolation, compounded by the expectations of widowhood from family and church. At the beginning of her mourning period, she wore the heavy widow's veil; and after the proper period, she was allowed into a lighter version. Her clothes went from black to gray and, at last, to white for summer. How long this decent mourning lasted I do not know, but however long, it was too long for Grandmother who, like Scarlett in *Gone With the Wind,* tapped her toes under her widow's weeds. She came again to live in her father's home along with my two-year-old father. They lived there until my father was eight.

Then scandal of scandals! Isaac Oliver had followed his brother to Tennessee and thought that eight years was long enough for Mattie to mourn. He proposed. Little Hope went wild with widow rules. Mattie was almost refused continued membership, not being the faithful widow of one husband. Also, she was riding her horse too fast for ladies, even though she did ride side-saddle. Amid this entire furor, she and Isaac rode to Adams, tied the knot, and St. Paul's following at Little Hope Church cooled off when Mattie and Isaac moved away to Kirkwood.

My father revered "Uncle Ike." As an old man, Uncle Ike's death brought tears in his voice as he recalled his step-father's instructions to him in his eighteenth year. He was to be responsible for his mother and half-sister. Grandmother kept the second set of widow's rules until my father married at thirty-four and brought my mother into the household. "One house is not big enough for two women and two women can't share one man," she declared. Therefore, she mailed a valentine.

There was a widower about a mile across the fields who could see my grandmother's lamp at night, shining in her upstairs bedroom window. After the valentine, he sent a note: "Mattie, if I can come calling, let your window shade up and down tonight." You know the rest. When Grandmother was fifty-four, I got the only grandfather I ever knew—Josephus King. Being a tobacco buyer, "Seph" moved Mattie into town and bought her a stucco house with bathroom! The great footed tub provided me my first town bath and water slide. A blood grandfather could not have been more patient and generous; and this same Josephus King was the true grandfather of Howard King, husband of Teena King of our congregation and also the grandfather of Jim Holleman of Conroy, Marable and Holleman.

Despite Paul's letter to Timothy, here was a romance I witnessed that waxed into genuine love. I believe our Christ would applaud the last years of my grandparents' delight in each other. St. Paul could soar so high into faith, into hope, into transcendence, yet descend so low into nit-picking hatefulness. And he did want the women in their place. If he had had a wife, his epistles no doubt would be vastly different, depending on the quality of the relationship. My grandmother would have done him good. Perhaps he would have waxed wanton for widows.

61

Dorothy Ann Ross Russo, daughter of the beloved Dr. John Ross, was my French teacher at Clarksville High School in 1939 and 1940. Having studied in France and just graduated from Vanderbilt, she came to us as a fresh French breeze, opening vistas and hopes for our unformed dreams.

Who ever heard of a "Tea Dance?" Miss Ross knew of such an occasion and we had such a dance—over the Coca-Cola bottling plant on North Second Street. The football heroes were goggle-eyed at her elegance and sophistication and adored her at a distance. John William Welker was so inspired by her that he became one of the outstanding French teachers in the Southeast and was awarded the Legion of Honor from the French government.

As we grow older, age differences seem to disappear. Dorothy Ann is seven years older than I, but through these many years together with our children and our trials and tribulations, we have become the fastest of friends. She has been my mentor into the world of ideas and influenced me away from pompous piety. What a difference one person can make in your life!

Dorothy Ann has always called me for domestic advice—cooking, cleaning, sewing, and other mundane matters. With such problems at hand, I introduced her to the *True Eye*, and we, with great pleasure, bequeath this treasure to the world at large.

> *The light of the body is the eye:*
> *If therefore thine eye is single,*
> *Thy whole body shall be full of light.*

Matthew 6:22

Dorothy Ann Russo and I have discovered a great legacy. It is a gift of the *True Eye*. This eye gives you complete confidence. It liberates you to tackle any job, takes down the mole-hill mountains, clears the path of any anticipated failure, allows you to size up a situation in one bold glance, and puts intrepid soles on faint-hearted feet.

There are no instructions too complex or measurements too intricate that the *True Eye* cannot eyeball them correctly. It demands no hedging around—hemming or hawing—just, "Do it!!"

Now this is a pearl-of-great-price, this single eye. I beheld it firsthand and have adopted it, however imperfectly, for my liberation and, lo, have passed it on to Dorothy Ann, one who gathered immediately to her bosom such an expeditious gift. How our lives have been simplified.

Miss Gloria Powers—Mrs. Abbot Powers—late of Kirkwood, was the possessor of this gift. She first came into my infant focus as I became a regular Sunday visitor in her household of ten children, ranging in ages from full-blown beards to unblown noses. Here there was delight in disorder, and order in chaos.

Miss Glory's confident true eye matched her size and her general bearing. From underneath her tent dress, cut butterfly, peeped cascades of corpulence that draped from her elbows and knees. Despite her face-lifting hairdo screwed to the top of her head, her great jowls shook with good humor and her voice, resonating on a bass line, quaked the pots in their stacks and tinkled the glasses. Her blue true eyes overlooked a W. C. Field's landscape, adorned at its end with her "seeing" glasses. Yet there was an elegance of lightness in her steps as she wove between the cook stove and the flour bin with a battalion's worth of biscuits. Her true eye measured the crowd, sifted several sifters of flour in a dishpan and made a hole in the center where she judged in lard and buttermilk. As if by magic, the biscuits were perfect.

All were welcome as we children made havoc through the house, jumping from the rafters in the attic and perusing old trunks for dress-up. There was never heard a discouraging word of "cool down, be quiet," or "straighten up your mess." She said children needed "imagination." My first exposure to dancing—that worldly pleasure—was from the Powers' parlor Victrola playing, "Yes, Sir, That's My Baby" while the grown children did the Charleston. Miss Glory had fringed the girls' skirts to accentuate the shimmy and, despite Baptist disputation, declared dancing part of "imagination."

After Miss Glory had fed the majority of the Intermediate Sunday School Class of Kirkwood Church, she blocked out Pandemonium, arranged her folds into a split hickory rocker, split just for her, and put on her "reading" glasses. Here she feasted her true eye. By Kirkwood standards she had a literary turn. She vowed that no one had any sense until they had read books. Her children's names reflected the scope of her eye. There was Brandon, Iris, Enoch, Beatrice, Hester, Arthur, Tess, Susana, Silas, and finally, Val Jean.

Miss Glory's husband, Mr. Abbot, was a small Pa Kettle of a man who looked to her for the final word on any subject. One wondered what small part he played in the creation of these ten children since he called her "Mama." When there was a calf to sell she would true eye it and without a moment's equivocation name its price; when there was an acreage to let, she immediately knew its terms; when the tobacco went to market, she set its price per pound and stuck with it. Within her household it was the same. Miss Glory could sit in her chair, eye a space, and wallpaper to fit; she could hold up dress fabric in the air and cut gores for skirts and enlarge armholes; in one afternoon she could cut and sew a change of clothes for every younger child in the household—all with her true eye. The marvel of it all was that her eye never seemed to fail.

As I look back on Miss Glory, I know she early came upon a great truth: the imperfection of perfection, or maybe, it should be the perfection of imperfection. She knew nothing could be perfect and you had to go on and do something, not be frozen in total paralysis trying to have everything just right. I would say she thought seventy-five per cent was most acceptable and with ten children she would probably accept sixty-five per cent. Her true eye told her the windows didn't have to be clean or the house dusted to have company. A relaxed good time and plenty of biscuits were much more important. Too, she knew someone had to have leadership and clarity of confidence to bring that big family through the depression; and since Mr. Abbot had neither, she made sure her children had an example of a single eye that filled the whole body with light and joy.

Dorothy Ann and I now can put our true eye on an undulating dress hem with utmost confidence, and there's no waistline too tight that we can't let it out—not to mention entertaining with all the dust nicely rearranged. We understand the *True Eye* and the truth is setting us free. Thank you, Miss Glory, for this glorious gift.

62

Life shouldn't be a journey to the grave with the intention of arriving safely in a pretty and well-preserved body, but rather to skid in broadside, thoroughly used up, totally worn out, and loudly shouting—Wow, what a ride! Thank you, Lord!!!

Quote handed to me by our very own, the Rev. Mickey Richaud

Ah, to skid into the grave broadside, perhaps knocking some carved angels from their pedestals and skewing the faux grass from the honest dirt. With no pickling juice in my veins, pat me quickly on the face with a shovel lest I reignite like the mythological Phoenix. "Wow, what a ride! Thank you, Lord."

Broadsiding must be in my genes. Pretty funeral parlors doings do not suit me—nor did they suit Aunt Ada Weems. For 82 years, she did a life long broadsiding, totally worn out, used up, and served out: four orphan children to help raise, including my mother; two stepdaughters and two children of her own; the first to be called to a birthing or the laying out of the dead; open arms to shelter a teenage girl, pregnant by her brother-in-law; and a 12-year stretch of caring for her mentally deranged husband who was reduced to an animal-like state, crawling about and fouling himself.

To quote the poet, she did not "rust unburnished, but shone with use."

When Aunt Ada came to die, she laid out her work clothes for the next day, got her palm-leaf fan in hand against the summer heat, laid her worn out body down and skidded gently into death and didn't disturb her sheets or counterpane.

Aunt Ada had planned well her journey to the grave: no long waiting and wailing, no embalming in that pickling juice, no preaching through the Pearly Gates—just a simple graveside service with a blind neighbor singing "Bless Be the Tie that Binds." The heavens wept for her. Cousin Billy Welker, Marcelite's husband, being a nephew, was a pallbearer; and this being the era of blue suede shoes, Cousin Billy had a new pair. They lost their suede in a loblolly of red clay. Aunt Ada literally skidded in broadside with the undertakers and pallbearers struggling in the Shiloh mud. What a life! What a death! What a love!

Over and against Aunt Ada's broadside skid is the narrow-sided, pretty and well-preserved arrival at the final portal. Wealthy Brazilian ladies are the master preservers. With my own eyes, I have beheld this. Jack says they have had so many facelifts that they are "possum-jawed" with an eternal thin-mouthed grin, topped by eyes, eternally surprised. Every hair, every fingernail, every errant mole, every fold of unfortunate flab has been rectified, and no natural childbirth has ever left the stretchable, stretched. All women of wealth have Caesareans.

One Brazilian lady, who visited us while her husband was buying Tennessee Walking Horses, could not get her heels to the ground. When I found her a pair of tennis shoes to wear to the stables to see their horses, she walked on tiptoes. Having worn extremely high heels for so many years, she found her leg tendons frozen in this position and they would not let her feet come down. While I was rattling her around in Jack's old farm truck with its stubborn clutch, I asked her if she drove a shift or an automatic, at which time she gave me a blank stare and replied, "I don't know; I have a chauffeur." Now that's traveling pretty! No broadsiding here.

Lory and Heinz Huyer, our Brazilian friends.

While visiting in Brazil some years ago, my wealthy friends took me up on a very high mountain to see the beauty of this magnificent country. What did I see? Just below us on the mountainside was a scene of the most abject poverty I had ever witnessed: hovels with only three sides, pregnant women with naked toddlers at their side, no visible sanitation, vultures on rubble heaps and on and on. These pretty and preserved people quoted "the poor always with us." How shall they answer Father Abraham? Who are their least brethren?

May I skid broadside in my grave—used up, burned out, given out to others, smiled out, wrinkled out, and lastly, loved out. Though I give my body to be burned, and have no love, the whole journey is a washout. Thank you, Lord, for the ride so far, and anytime there is a blowout, I'll depend on your mercy for a safe entry.

63

Behold, God will not cast away a perfect man, neither will he help the evil doers; till he fill thy mouth with laughing and thy lips with rejoicing.

Job 8

My grandmother, Martha Elizabeth Winn, was a *Fundamentalist*. She, like my daddy, loved a practical joke, a good story—often quite spicy—and both of them could spot phonies from Port Royal to Kirkwood with a special eye for shyster preachers. I do believe they went to church for their general amazement and amusement, which filled their mouths with laughing at the foibles from the pulpit and the pews.

There appeared at Little Hope Baptist Church one revivalist hungry for more than fried chicken. Announcing early on that the Lord had sent him to blot out the vanities of the flesh at Little Hope, he, like St. Paul, condemned elaborate hairdos and only approved of modest coiffures, parted in the middle and severely bunned at the back. Anything more was of the Devil. Now my grandmother was considered quite a beauty in her day, her hair being her joy and crown; and the fiery brother's eyes flashed often into her pew with much desire for her immortal soul or mortal otherwise. She once warned us girls, "Remember, preachers have all their principal parts." A wise grammar lesson.

Thus grandmother's preacher story began: "That old farce bragged that whatever page he opened in the Bible that he could bring his fingers down on a verse that would be the very text that someone in the congregation needed to save their soul. 'The Holy Spirit guides me.' He flopped open the Bible, squinted down at the page where I knew he had his finger already fixed and read Matthew the twenty-fifth chapter, the seventeenth verse, one of those red-lettered Christ verses, "Let him which is on the housetop not come down…"

Grandmother heated up, "That old Bible baloney salesman looked square at me, did a few hmmmms, some chicken-stuffed grumps, pulled his galluses out, snapped them a time or two and announced his text: 'Top Knot Come Down.' I may be adding a letter of the alphabet but the Spirit is speaking to some sinner here tonight."

Grandmother always told us children, "I was never vain about my beauty," but she did pile her thick chestnut hair high on her head, put the curling iron down the lamp chimney, and made a most appealing row of ringlets across her forehead and dangled careless curls in front of her ears and at the nape of her neck. This was worldly stuff! Almost more than the Lord's anointed could bear. Also she "rooged" her cheeks and "chalked" her face, the sign of the harlot, according to this preacher, along with the top-knot that wouldn't come down.

"Harlotry and vanities of the flesh do not see the resurrection of the righteous, only the condemnation of the damned," as my grandmother was pinpointed.

She waited her turn after preaching. With a twinkle after the passing of those many years, she ended the story, "I told that preacher my hair had already been resurrected and if I am a harlot, you are worse to be lusting after harlots; and if you don't quit looking at my legs through my petticoat when I am carrying my lantern and getting up on my horse, there isn't going to be enough of you to resurrect." She said Cuddin' Lula Highsmith agreed,

"Glory to God for you, Mattie." So much for Little Hope's sexual harassment and women's lib.

Grandmother's *Fundamentalism* has carried me far. It has carried me away from literalism and legalism into the freedom of love and grace. I bless this gene that comes from her. This legacy has seen me up from many deaths—deaths almost too dark to face in the early morning's light, death of dreams and hopes, death that took hold of my physical body, the death of relationships that withered in anger and bitter unforgiveness, and the death from doubt—to curse God and die.

Easter is about rising, a levitation that defied earthbound gravity and causes one to come up out of death; and surely the word levity has the same etymological root. From out of the depths of my darkest of deaths, there has come a spark, a light, a resurrection of laughter from a place beyond my knowing. The Biblical account of Christ's resurrection and his first meeting with his apostles has a somber and mystical note. But if the writers of these accounts could have gone back some seventy or eighty years to the actual scene, I can imagine the joy, the tears, the laughter, the forgiveness, and the fun that they would surely have recorded.

The Christ who is our salvation and who is living in us has a sense of humor. He has gone before us and is preparing a place for us, and like Brer Rabbit in the *Tales of Uncle Remus*, I'm sure we will find our "laughing place" there.

64

You don't miss the music until the sweet song bird has flown.

An old adage my mother often quoted.

Sometime this song bird—or raucous crow—feels as though she should fly away forever from *Cumberland Lore*, silencing too many years of squawking. But, Gentle Reader, there are those who insist that I continue to inundate you with wandering wit, some wisdom, and often some worthless words. So what shall it be for August? Tiring from coming down from Mr. Olympus, the muses abandon me to "woolgathering." So woolgathering it shall be—maybe "three bags full."

My mother was an orphan woolgatherer. When she was 8 years-old she went to live part time with Grandma Wickham who kept a flock of sheep. This flock left tufts of wool in bushes, briar patches and in fence rows, and Grandma, being forever frugal, sent my mother out with a bag to gather this wool.

My mother recounted her respect and awe of her ancient grandmother. In the winter they sat in front of the fire and "carded" the wool. Carding was the process of combing the wool between two nail-studded boards to get the burrs out and to get the fibers running in the same direction in preparation for spinning the wool into thread. Can we, in 2007, imagine such?

Grandma Wickham, who had reared 10 children—Tanner Wickham being her youngest—was a semi-invalid, but Mama had such respect for her that whatever chore she was told to do she did as though Grandma were standing at her side. Upstairs was impossible for this matriarch. "Make sure you dust the battens of the doors, Maude," and Mama said she never neglected one batten even though she knew her grandmother could never climb the stairs.

When grandma died, my mother lived with Uncle John, Aunt Ada, and finally at Aunt Emma's who was the late John William Welker's mother and Marcelite's mother-in-law. At each place, she was well initiated into the work ethics of a poor, but proud people, and she learned skills from soap making to sewing a fine seam. Aunt Ada taught her that. At Aunt Emma's in Erin, she learned the King's English at a female academy, and at eighteen, passed the test to become a Montgomery County schoolteacher—in a one-room school, no less. When she married my daddy, she finally had a home of her very own, and to this home she brought skills that her generation passed on to me. I can't make soap, but I can make souse.

"Idle hands are the devil's workshop," so my mother quoted. From our 21st century perspective, where are the opportunities for workshops in cities, in subdivisions, in the crowded clangor of our days? Where is pioneer-type work, when every luxury and labor-saving device is at our elbows, instant entertainment at the press of a button, and food and clothing so abundant that we stuff ourselves and our closets with no effort?

We are in the midst of revolution that is beyond understanding, beyond our mortal knowing, into the transcendent. We have become woolgatherers, grasping for meaning, searching for ourselves in every fencerow and wayside bush. Where can we spin the fragile threads of our lives in this maddening rush of the 21st century? Where can we find solace away from the tyranny of possessions, the glorification of the self, and our pursuit of happiness? Where can we as a nation find ourselves away from solutions by war and the murder of neighbors?

This is woolgathering at its worst, thoughtless butchering of cultures we do not understand and disregarding histories we have never read. Our woolgathering is complete. We reap what we do not know.

Grandpaw Wickham had his last picture made holding his Bible on his knee and Grandma Wickham had her last picture made holding Grandpaw's picture on her knee and surrounded by their children. I can hear Grandpaw read: "I know my own and my own know me, as the Father knows me and I know the Father: and I lay down my life for the sheep." May all of us woolgatherers rest in these words.

65

My bounty is as boundless as the sea,
My love as deep; the more I give to them
The more I have, for both are infinite.

From Shakespeare's, Romeo and Juliet

This is February, the month of the valentine. How is your love thermometer and are you as love-struck as Romeo and Juliet? I dredge through family love stories to come up with real life romances that I knew, romances that endured and gave and gave and kept giving to the end. Mama's sister, Ada Livingston and her husband, David McBryde Austin, are the subjects of this February recounting.

Three orphaned little girls from the environs of Palmyra, Shiloh and Hackberry had their lives before them. Their chances were small but there were big hearts around them. Their Aunt Emma, Billy Welker's mother and Marcelite Welker's mother-in-law, took them into her already large family where they found schooling in some academy that no doubt had excellent teachers. What grammarians all three girls became. At eighteen, each sister passed the required test to become Montgomery County rural school teachers.

Ada Livingston's best friend was Mary Fessey of the Fessey clan at Hackberry. She too had passed the qualifying test, and these young girls were quite often courted by the young swains in their assigned communities. Mary Fessey must have had the Ringgold School because she soon caught the eye of Winfield Durrett, the father of Doctor Dawson Durrett and the grandfather of Mary Fessey Hackney. Before settling down, Mary and Ada decided they needed an adventure, somehow to see the world away from the hills and hollows of lower Montgomery County, to try their wings in another place. After answering an ad in a teachers' journal, they took off to Maxton, a small, sandy coastal town in North Carolina, where they signed a year's contract to teach. After

Relatives & Acquaintances

a year, Mary felt the need to go back home and nail Winfield down for good since he was waiting for her. Ada was unattached.

During the early twentieth century era, the local lady teachers took a room with a family and were integrated into their customs and routines and were admonished and advised by the mother of the household about their correct behavior and who was who in the community. Such was Aunt Ada's landlady.

The remainder of this account is from Aunt Ada's own remembrances. "McBryde Austin came calling and took me for a ride in his buggy. He was not handsome, rather ungainly, wore glasses and had a wide floppy mouth. I was most indifferent and unimpressed."

After not having many callers and having given a negative report on McBryde Austin, her landlady came on the scene and told Aunt Ada that she had rejected one of the finest of men whose family was respected far and wide for their scholarship and integrity. One cousin was the dean of Flora McDonald College at Red Springs and her sister, the Latin professor there. As to McBryde himself, he owned a drugstore, was an up-and-coming business man with farm property and other holdings. Possessions do brighten romance. McBryde did have courtly manners, a rarely fine horse and buggy, and his mouth didn't seem so broad anymore.

Aunt Ada told me that she dressed up in her best and found some pretense to go to the drugstore where she told Uncle Mac that she hadn't seen much of him lately. This broke the ice. He came a-courtin' in earnest.

Uncle Mac and his family came to Tennessee for the wedding, held in my parents' parlor. He wanted Ada's family to join in the joy of this occasion, and it was a long trip by train from Maxton by way of Atlanta to Clarksville. Thus began a love story in which one great soul gave and gave and loved and loved through many adversities with never a word of complaint nor criticism, only a recounting of his great fulfillment in his Ada.

By many standards, Aunt Ada was not a housekeeper. She was a student and a dreamer. But thanks to Uncle Mac there was always household help and he thought that gave her time for mothering his children and he still wept at the loss of their first born—a son. He honored the sacrifice of childbearing. There were two daughters to follow this great loss in his life.

After being a drugstore owner and such a loving and giving man, he was called "Dr. Austin" by the poor peoples around him and they came for medical advice and medication. He could patiently listen, give them his best diagnoses, and sell or give them over-the-counter medications. For the truly ill, he saw that they had the local doctor's attention. At Uncle Mac's funeral, the minister quoted King David when he heard that his general, Abner, had been killed in battle—"Know ye not that this day a prince and a great man has fallen in Israel?" That was McBryde Austin.

After his death, Aunt Ada venerated his legacy and said what a tragedy and void would have been in her life if she had rejected him because of his looks. She knew what a privilege it was to have been thus adored by someone who overlooked every flaw and somehow turned every fault into a beauty of character. "Ada has such a fine mind; she's so proud of my people; she cooks such lacey hoecakes and lady peas; she's such a steady driver." Was there never a negative thought?

It is so easy to find fault. It's a wonder my husband hasn't gotten rid of me long ago, but like Uncle Mac, he has turned many negatives into positives. On my side, I shall state that I haven't done much with his hard head. What truly goes on in our insides, only God and we know—sometimes we don't know, don't have a clue about ourselves. Was Uncle Mac an exception?

All our struggles with living together in relationships boils down to the same resolution: the more I give the more I have. It's the gospel, forever new. We are loved, accepted and forgiven because of God's unimaginable gift of Grace. It is our call to pass this good news on, not only to our mates, our family and friends, but to the whole world. "For God so loved the world…" This love is infinite. It's the love that will not let us go. This is our blessed assurance.

66

For unto us a child is born, unto us a son is given, and the government shall be upon his shoulders.

Isaiah 9

St. Valentine's Day is upon us. This day brings to mind a genuine fairy tale told to us by Aunt Ada Weems. She was a romanticist who wove into plot the intricacies of true-love-will-win-out with fair maiden, stern parent, noble farm boy and wise counselor. We children sat, spellbound, even though we had heard the story of Cousin Hugh Dunbar during every summer's visit. Aunt Ada would sigh, take a dip of snuff, turn her gray eyes toward the horizon as though she were telling this classic fairy tale for the first time.

The narrative began: "Cousin Hugh owned most of the Yellow Creek bottoms in the community, and his corn crops were the envy of all the hillside folks. He got more land and more crops and built himself a two-story house with porches upstairs and down, and an ice house, a blacksmith shop and six big barns. Even his little daughter, Hannah Marie, had her own playhouse with a tiny dinner bell and a fireplace that worked."

Aunt Ada's cousin had been a widower for sometime, and he, along with Uncle Will and Aunt Sook, delighted in Hannah's every move and desired for her all advantages. Mr. Hugh hired a governess who knew a smattering of Latin and had a speaking acquaintance with parsing. But she did not suffice. In Nashville, Hugh looked for a "finishing school" with exposure to the right people because he desired a proper son-in-law for well-bred grandchildren; yes, grandchildren!

Relatives & Acquaintances

According to Aunt Ada, Hannah, however, was difficult to "finish," preferring to ride her horse and stay in the fields with Uncle Will and the other farm hands. She was not finished enough for Nashville society and too finished for Palmyra and found no proper suitor. Cousin Hugh looked on in anguish. His heart yearned for his daughter's suitable marriage and grandsons to carry on his name.

Aunt Ada's eyes would soften as she got to the heart of her fairy story—the hero comes on the scene, love-conquers-all, the happy ending. This hero was a horse wrangler, a stalwart farm hand with lean and lithe good looks, who had all the skills that Hannah admired in a man. He can plow a mule with one line and never disturb a blade of corn. He "sets his saddle" like I've never seen before...All this got back to her father.

You know the plot: Promptly Jim Dunwoodie was banished from Hugh's kingdom, but he could not banish Jim from Hannah's heart. There were clandestine meetings and desperate partings, leaving Hannah pale and withdrawn. Uncle Will was privy to the situation. He gave Jim his best counsel: "Mr. Hugh he mighty hard and sot in his ways, but there ain't nothing he crave more than a grandchilde. There ain't no way out but you and Miss Hannah slip off and tie the knot and you get your wife with child as soon as you are man enough. Then with Miss Hannah holdin' a chile under her heart, that man will sho' melt."

There was a long silence and rejection from Hugh as Hannah and Jim settled into a modest house some miles away where he was farm manager. It was said through the community that her father disinherited Hannah and had forbade her to set foot on his property. But "a little child shall lead them." When he heard the baby's name was Hugh Dunbar, he saddled his horse, praised God for his grandson and rode the miles for a joyous and tearful reconciliation.

Uncle Will's advice was the happy ending. Half the kingdom was Jim Dunwoodie's, and eventually all of it came to Hannah and their sons and daughters. The governing of Cousin Hugh's estate rested on these grandchildren's shoulders, and I personally know of their progeny who have carried on their great-grandfather's tradition of being true husbandmen of their fields.

So for St. Valentine's Day is there a greater gift than sons and daughters? Who can guess what they shall be?

As I watched George W. Bush take his oath of office on the same Bible that George Washington used, and I recalled the generations of president-sons that have come and gone during this span of time, I was awed by the governments that have been on their shoulders. When a son was given to Nancy Hanks, what if she could have known who this was and what he would be?

All our sons and daughters are miracles, and I marvel at their creativity and diversity, knowing how poor I would be without them. Grandchildren are a different, but no less, treasure. Perhaps I shall not see the government that will rest on their shoulders, but I have faith that the times will be in good hands.

67

Tis an old said saw. Children and fools speak true.

John Lyly

You know where the "Springfield-Ashland City" exit is on the interstate. When my granddaughter, Eleanor, Charles and Elizabeth's daughter, was old enough to be separated from her mother, she came to this exit to meet me. How I looked forward to these visits. With her favorite toys in hand and her mother's carefully packed bag, she came ready for most anything—her particular passions being cookie baking, tea parties under the staircase, and Cinderella. As she grew older and learned to read, it was a book—*A Thousand and One Questions, Riddles, and Funny Jokes*. She had read *The Cat in the Hat* until she knew every word and you didn't dare leave anything out. If you missed a page or were in a hurry or sleepy, she would stop you. "Granny, you left out..." and she would pick up the line. What fun! And how I craved a nap after lunch.

You are my sweetheart, my everything wished for and everything hoped for. You are my precious Eleanor.

Back to our routine. Eleanor was about three years old and a little more, when we started this routine of flour, sugar, and all the ingredients so demanded. She knew every one. She watched the mighty stirrings and sifting, the added ingredients as their turn came, and actually helped some with dropping the cookies on the pans for the oven. As she grew older, she helped with all phrases of this daring adventure. Always, she stood in a chair, reversed, and dictated the proceedings, but once she was too far from the stove and at just the right angle to lose the center of gravity and tipped the chair over. Ka Boom! Such crying and outrage! She wasn't hurt, but her command post had been compromised and she never trusted it again. Remember, she was growing all the while.

Forever the tease, Daddy Jack would come through the kitchen from time to time to steal cookies. Eleanor watched him and the cookies like they were rare jewels. She would get disinterested in her patrolling after some time, and Daddy Jack would get two cookies. "Yum-yum, these cookies are sure good." In his defense, he told her he had paid for the flour and sugar to make the cookies, but this wasn't good enough for Eleanor. The cookies were hers.

Enough of cookie-baking. It's on to Cinderella. From the rag bag, I chose the worst-looking clothes I could find, got a mop and small broom that were handy, and a cudgel to beat poor Cinderella. We were ready. With mop and pail in hand and a most pitiful look on her face, Cinderella had to face the cruel stepmother, who at this point, was screeching her commands.

Cinderella chose the toilet to clean. Why she chose this spot above all spots, I do not know; but she told me I was not being mean enough. "Granny, this is the real thing. You've got to be tough."

She stayed in character as long as it suited her, and I was exhausted from being the wicked stepmother until her attention was drawn to something less austere. However, the rich prince with the glass slipper never came and I put her Cinderella clothes in storage, along with her kite.

What tea parties we had underneath the stair case. The steps went up to one level, turned a corner, and proceeded to the top floor, leaving a space underneath with two doors—one in the hallway and the other one in the bathroom. What privacy unless the latch was fastened on the bathroom side! Anyway, we cleared out the boots and canned tomatoes and put in two small chairs and table for a perfect spot for a tea party. There was a great finishing touch: A sign which read, "No Boys Allowed." Eleanor was the warden. Daddy Jack was the one who tried to get in, making out with a chair to sit down, all the while saying how much he liked cookies. Eleanor threw a fit. If he had gotten in, there was no place for him to sit, and he had had the fun, listening to her great protestations.

After a morning of cookie-baking and Cinderella, it was nap time for Granny. How I longed for this respite, this reprieve from all the hurly-burly of the morning with lunch to fix and my families' usual needs. The bed looked so good. Eleanor in the meantime had grown to five and she could already read! That was a help. Out came the book, *The Thousand and One Things* to ask a riddle to enjoy or a plain joke. At first, I could cooperate but as time grew deeper, I would almost fall asleep and didn't respond. "Granny, you are going to sleep. Just one more and I will be through." I never heard her. She too had a long nap; in fact, I was awake and up and doing before she was.

Now Eleanor is in school fulltime and my time with her got farther and farther apart as she takes her place among her peers. She is perhaps the finest violinist anywhere, near or far, for her age group. Needless to say, I will go to any length to hear her play. I will always go back to those early years, before she could read, before she could judge teasing from reality, before she was judged by grown-up rules, and I know this saying is profound: "Children and fools speak true."

68

I am certain of nothing but the heart's affection and the truth of imagination.

John Keats

"Ah ha, she's graduated." Dare I tell you of Eleanor Marshall's accomplishments? You will think I am bragging, making it up. From the cookie making, the tea parties, to the pursuits of academe, I shall take you on a ride and I do not exaggerate. She, like all grandchildren, is an exception to the rules, and, unlike all other grandchildren, is unique in her own world. She was and is smart and I do mean just that. Where she got her brains, I'll never know. Certainly it wasn't from our son, Charles, or anyone on our side of the family; so, Elizabeth, you get the credit. You are the one who made Eleanor so smart.

Her first schooling was at the University School, a part of Vanderbilt, where she assisted her teacher by helping some of the students with their studies. She knew her lessons already and was looking for something to do. What a help to have a student teacher.

Along with this was violin lessons that made me think of Isaac Stern. Now, wasn't this a stretch of imagination?

Charles and Elizabeth knew they had something rare in Eleanor, and they determined to send her to the best schools. As a high schooler, she applied to Phillip's Academy at Andover, Massachusetts, where, with her records, she was easily accepted. At first, the up-Easterners laughed at her Southern accent; but before long they didn't laugh anymore because of her leading all the classes. When she graduated she was head of her class in the liberal arts and finished in 2002, *summa cum laude.*

Now where to go to college. Eleanor made application to the main Ivy-league colleges—Harvard, Yale, Princeton, University of Chicago, Stanford, and on-and-on. She was accepted by one and all, hands down, with offers of scholarships, if needed. She is the only person I know who turned down Harvard twice—she chose Yale instead. It was the same story. She was the helper of students who needed work in whatever discipline they were weakest in, and she made them work or she didn't fool with them. It was the same story with more honors added: Phi Beta Kappa and *summa cum laude*. She graduated from Yale in 2006.

Eleanor wanted to be a doctor. She applied to the right schools again—Harvard, Yale, Stanford, and I don't know who else. Here is where she turned down Harvard for the second time. She didn't want anymore "up-east" matriculation. She wanted sunshine, beautiful blooms, and exotic plantings, along with the best college of medicine. She chose Stanford, as far away from the Eastern seaboard as she could get; besides, they gave her a full scholarship based on her need to do research. In the meantime, in preparation for the labs, she had to do all the pre-medicine routine as everyone else. After two years, she gave up on the "research project," finding out she was more of a people-person, enjoying the cases assigned to her. Eleanor will graduate from med-school in 2011, and there is another chapter awaiting her. She is to be married!

Relatives & Acquaintances

Eleanor with her parents, Elizabeth and Charles Marshall, at her graduation from Yale.

The wedding? Next September! Eleanor was never "boy-crazy" and, in particular, didn't like blind dates. One of her friends wanted her to meet this young man, a Southerner, from Memphis. She finally gave in and with much reluctance went along just to satisfy the girl and to have a night out. You know the rest. Eric Osborne has graduated from Stanford Law School and at present is working for a Federal Judge in Memphis. If this separation can bear the strain, you will know that it is true love. Then he is assured of an opening in a law firm in Washington, D.C., and Eleanor hopes to find a residency there. Such are the aspirations of young people. I wish them well.

From the cookie-making, Cinderella days, to the graduation from Stanford med school is a long haul. I've always told Eleanor she was the sweetest, finest, most beautiful girl in the whole world, and that is true. Despite her fine mind, you would never guess, on first meeting her, that she wasn't just an ordinary pretty girl. She declines all make-up, just a natural beauty without any store-bought embellishments.

So, Dr. Marshall, your Granny is so proud of you, so pleased with you, so prone to mention your name that I feel grateful to have you in the family. But you are my sweetheart, my everything wished for and everything hoped for. You are my precious Eleanor.

69

There are two things you can't move:
A tom cat and an old woman

My husband

Meta Killebrew Silvey tells the tale of her tom cat. One of the children, I don't know which one, was moving to Fayetteville, Arkansas, and picked up old Tom, put him in a cage, hauled him across the Cumberland, the Tennessee, and finally the Mississippi Rivers. How's that for moving a tom cat! About six months later, who but old Tom would be sitting on Meta's back porch, meowing away for his breakfast, a meal he got first thing every morning. Now that's a traveling cat, a cat who can swim, walk, or hitch-hike a ride across three rivers and back home to Rossview. He seemed little worse for the wear and picked up his normal routine, watching for mice and being a general nuisance.

Now an old woman is different. She can move, but it is with much protestation—"where will I put Aunt Polly's picture or my easy chair," or, "where will Hyman leave his dirty boots," and on-and on. I speak here of Miss Lizzie Welsh and Mr. Hyman Welch as they got ready to leave the old Nichols place down on Red River and move up on Rossview Road to the "bug house." Mr. Joe Milan was our local arthropodic expert, and due to the passing of time had to give up his bug hunt and retire, leaving his stone house to new owners, the Welches.

Now it was quite a drive from the Nichols' place, up from the lowlands of Red River to the higher ground of Rossview. Miss Lizzie had stayed until the last load was ready, all personal items of great worth to her and under her personal care and protection. The main part of the moving had been done by truck with burly young men to load and unload, but this last load was under her watchful eye on a wagon, pulled by Mr. Hyman's faithful old tractor, with him as navigator. The last thing aboard was Miss Lizzie's easy chair, and she was to ride in it, watching with great care all the items on the load.

Now you would say that Mr. Hyman was hard-of-hearing; but I would say he was deaf. He couldn't hear thunder. Too, he was absent-minded and dwelt in the land of poetry, of ideas, of things too deep for the ordinary brain of the local-yokels. He was a scholar by heredity and by his own introspection. For Rossview Road, he was flat smart. He was in charge of the tractor and the wagon with his wife's priceless load, all the way from the Nichols' place to their new home, which was about three miles. "Good-bye" to the old place and soon to be "hello" to the new.

Miss Lizzie got on the back of the wagon in her easy chair, reared back, and put herself facing the road behind her. "This is going to be an easy ride," she thought, as Mr. Hyman took his place as the one driver to their new home. With much smoking and choking, the old tractor got tuned just right and with a mighty jerk, a jerk felt all the way to Red River, got them going up-hill in the right direction. But horror of horrors! The mighty jerk had turned Miss Lizzie over backwards with her feet and behind the only portion of her anatomy showing to any trailing vehicle. She screamed, she hollowed, she, being rather round and "fleshy" couldn't get up, and Mr. Hyman never once looked back. Mr. Hyman being deaf and totally unaware never bothered to check his load.

Miss Lizzie was a real comic. She could tell this story with her eyes dancing and everyone all ears. With dark curly hair, a round face and a rounder body, she was of the funny paper. She chuckled all the while she was telling this tale of their move in 1960. If you hadn't guessed, this was Bobby Welch's mother. He was away, married to Mary Emma, and missed her traveling story. Trigg Welsh, Bobby's brother, was living with his parents when they left the Nichols' house on Red River and moved to the "bug house" because it was near the road and was tighter than the old log house, built in 1790, or thereabouts.

Later Trigg married a lovely woman and brought her into the family circle. As I write this, Mary Emma and Bobby have renovated the Nichols' place, made it into a refuge, and they spend much of their time there with children and grandchildren up for the weekend.

Home is where you hang your hat! Not so. Home is the place where you have put all your hopes, your treasures, and even your soul. As an old woman, I have moved after fifty plus years, and I know the agony of leaving a place behind. But I console myself. Home has become the place that is not built with hand, but, by faith, we shall be at Home.

SAINTS

70

Cast your bread on the waters, for you will find it after many days.

Ecclesiastes 11:1

Who among us is old enough to remember the original "Care Package?" The word has gotten into our vernacular and has come to mean any package sent away to poor relations, college students, various church-related mission groups, and yes, to our children who crave our bags of garden freshness and real smokehouse sausage.

From whence this care package and what is it etymology? During World War II and before our nation became embroiled in this battle against Fascist Germany, we as a nation were asked to help the British, being so small in number and struggling to keep their country alive. We were a lifeline against hunger and cold. All their resources were going to the war effort as the civilian population suffered—little food, little clothing, and at times little hope with the bombing and burning of their cities. Hitler was determined to break this brave island's spirit. You know Winston Churchill's response!

Across the Atlantic the "Care Package" came alive. Caring persons could choose a family in Britain and were given their name and address. When the American found out the family's makeup, they could start getting a monthly package on its way. Who among us but Trinity Episcopal Church's own Helen Danforth Ross, Dorothy Ann Russo's mother, in her usual fast-forward fashion got the ball rolling for her chosen family, a family of Thitheringtons, who lived in Liverpool. The family was a mother with four boys and the father away at war. Having known Granny Ross, I can see her in my mind's eye, making every consideration for these boys: shoe sizes, shirts, socks, underwear, tablets and drawing supplies, and for the mother whatever food stuff she was allowed to send. There could be no perishables, but Helen Danforth of New England stock was thorough and determined, sending oatmeal, beans, and stick-to-the-ribs items. There were some chocolates too—maybe hidden in the oatmeal. For eight to ten years, up into the 50s, Granny Ross sent these monthly "Care Packages" and corresponded with Mrs. Thitherington, meeting as many needs for her and her sons as she could provide. Her husband had been wounded in the war.

Now to make a long story longer, Granny Ross did indeed cast her "bread wide upon the waters;" and her daughter, Dorothy Ann, and granddaughter, Hedy, found it returned "after many days." They found this bread returned by the way of the BBC—British Broadcasting Corporation. One Stephen Thitherington arrived at Rossview on the 3rd of October. He was in charge of the BBC US08 election bus.

To quote his schedule: "Starting in L.A. on 10 September, the BBC US08 election bus will travel through fifteen states before ending in New York on 17 October. BBC reporters will discover what Americans are really talking about, and what the world is saying about their nation."

After his father's death, Stephen found six letters from Helen Ross to Isabella Thitherington in his father's papers. Stephen longed to connect with the Ross family and farm and to say "thank you." Therefore, in planning the itinerary of the BBC US08 election bus tour, Stephen had included an overnight stop in Clarksville/Ft. Campbell, KY, enroute from the presidential debates in St. Louis to Nashville. In his possession he had letters from Mrs. Helen Ross, Rt. 3, Clarksville, Tennessee, and he hoped against hope that he might find some descendents of this beloved Mrs. Ross.

Calling *The Leaf Chronicle,* Stephen got the name of Ann Ross, Helen Ross's niece, and right away she gave him Dorothy Ann Ross Russo's number, who at 93 is Helen's only living child. Hedy (Helen), Dorothy Ann's daughter, was there where this fantastic story brings the "bread cast on the waters" home.

Stephen and the huge BBC bus were staying at a local motel where Hedy picked him up and took him to their farm for a long visit. It was love at first sight: the farm, Dorothy Ann's unique house with her husband's paintings and sculptures all around, Hedy's gourmet supper served on Helen Ross's museum dishes, and then Hedy's reading her grandmother's correspondence to Stephen's grandmother. This was tear-jerking stuff. With her early bedtime forgotten, Dorothy Ann was up until 11 o'clock basking in the joy of her mother's legacy of love and service.

What a denouement to this miracle story! The next morning Stephen and that monstrous BBC bus with its load of correspondents from many points of the globe—even Afghanistan—came to meet Dorothy Ann and record her on tape. The bus was too big for her narrow lane so the driver parked in a pasture close to her house and she arrived by wheelchair. Hedy was also interviewed and taped, and on Tuesday, the day of the debates at Belmont College, she was invited to lunch in Nashville with Stephen and a top BBC reporter, Allan Little.

Stephen Titherington says he shall return. He now lives near London and is an administrator with the BBC. Helen Ross's bread cast on the waters is still rippling, flowing, returning, and her kindness and unique visions of casting bread live on in many hearts. Let us go and do likewise.

71

I know not when my Lord may come
At night or noonday fair,
Or if I walk the vale with him
Or meet him in the air.

An old Baptist hymn

Dorothy Ann Russo has been intrigued to know about the eschatological (theological dealings with the last things) writings which foretell Christ's second coming. Part of these teachings is known in some denominations as the "Rapture," the literal taking up of the "saved" here on earth who will meet our Lord in the sky. Woe to those left behind!

Having already written about Uncle Warner Winn who had all the pronouncements from the Gospels, the Epistles, and the Revelation of John pinpointed, I shall share again his expected rapture. Not being overly fond of soap and water and overly fond of tobacco juice, he figured out the exact day of the rapture, shaved, took a bi-yearly bath, shined his shoes, put on his suit and rocked on the front porch, waiting to be taken up to meet the Lord upon his second coming. Sunset found him saying that he had miscalculated by a century and the rapture would be in the year 2000. "Somehow I missed it."

Uncle Warner had Christ's own words to back him up. From Matthew's Gospel: "But of that day and that hour no man knoweth, no man, no, not the angels of heaven, but the Father only…Then shall two be in a field; the one shall be taken and the other left. Two women shall be grinding at the mill; the one shall be taken, the other left. Watch therefore, for you know not what hour your Lord doth come."

In 1 Thessalonians, St. Paul writes: "For the Lord himself shall descend from heaven with a shout, with the voice of the archangel, and with the trump of God: and the dead in Christ shall rise first. Then we which are alive and remain shall be caught up together in the clouds, to meet the Lord in the air, and so we shall ever be with the Lord."

Being "raptured" has gotten into verb form and is sung by my Pentecostal friends with much fervor—"I'll Fly Away."

Never have I heard a sermon at Trinity on being raptured. Kirkwood did not leave me so uninformed. With warnings from the pulpit of all the sins of our earthly flesh, I feared with the sound of the trumpet and the Lord descending, I would be left behind. No flying away in the air for me. If I were at the movie, no wings; if we were slipping cigarettes behind the barn; no wings; if

I had on shorts, a disgrace to the Lord in the sky; if I were found courting in Lover's Lane, I may have flown a little bit but in the wrong direction.

In the congregation of our church, I picked out some saintly souls who I thought eligible to be raptured: one sparrow of a woman with watery eyes and properly pursed lips who never spoke above a monotone of properness and piety; an old gentleman, bent on a honeysuckle-entwined walking stick, so blind that he attempted to eat a paper plate that held his Sunday-dinner-on-the-grounds-pie. The preacher was in doubt. How could he fly away with his 60 inch girth and his 300 pounds that could hardly mount the pulpit?

The Uncle Warner type "saints," knowledgeable about every minute nuance of the Gospels, the Epistles, and lastly, the Revelation of John (the Apocalypse) have all this magnificent poetic imagery figured out. They know the numbers for the rapture. John, on the rocky isle of Patmos, recorded his visions and uses much of the prophetic symbolism of the books of Daniel and Ezekiel. The Jews knew these figures of speech. The great whore, according to most scholars of the Revelation, is reference to the Roman Empire.

After all the beasts, the opening of the books, the damnations to the lake of fire, and the glories of heaven and the agonies of hell, John concludes his revelation with these words of Jesus: "I, Jesus, have sent my angel to you with this testimony for the churches. I am the root and offspring of David, the bright and morning star. The Spirit and the Bride say 'come.' Let him who is thirsty come, let whosoever will take the water of life without price."

In the chorus, the old hymn concludes with Paul's words: "I know in whom I have believed and am persuaded that he is able to keep that which I have committed unto him against that day."

To fly or not to fly—not to worry!

72

*Thou hast been faithful over a few things;
I will make thee ruler over many things . . .*

Matthew 25:23

Saints? Who are they? The first one who comes to my mind is our long-ago hired hand. He was one of the tall African tribes, stately and austere, and in retrospect, our "Uncle Thomas" sounds patronizing, but that is what we children called him. When I first remember him in the late 1920s, he was in his 60s, no doubt born into slavery or just after Emancipation. Recounting his life's history, he always told of his childhood spent in the fields with his mother who must have instilled in this little boy the mystery and majesty of God and His creation.

Thomas Moody was a poet. He may have been illiterate—I don't know—but a literacy of spirit had been breathed into his being that no tutoring could impart. The black church was about a half-mile as the crow flies behind our house. My father, Bracy Oliver, even though a born Southerner, never knew anything about segregation, and we would go to Foston Springs to hear the preaching and singing. Invariably, the preacher called on Tom Moody to pray. From thence we were transported on a voice, resounding and prophetic, as he extolled the glories of the heavens, the vastness of the teeming seas, the mystery of God's stooping to salvage sinful man, the assurance of our place in the "house with many mansions," and the goodness of life and the joy of being a lamb washed in the blood.

This lamb had meager pasture, indeed, and how easily his prayers could have been selfish petitions rather than soaring praise. When as a child I first remember Uncle Thomas and Aunt Quance, they lived in a one-room cabin with a lean-to where she spent her days alone in bed. She had been an invalid for years. Each morning before coming for his day's work, he tended her needs with utmost care and patience, meticulously arranging her bed and food so she could care for herself during the day. Then upon his homecoming from the fields, there was her bath, the laundry in the washtubs at night, and the preparation of food again for the next day. Always there were starched pillowcases and newspaper "lace" on the mantel piece. This he did for many years, alone, since they had no children. He never wavered once in his faithfulness; he had taken his vows for better or worse.

After Quance left for the house with many mansions and Thomas had retired, he would call on my father. Stately, in his best clothes and watch fob, he commanded respect; and even before the day of civil rights and our awareness of the indignities we had done to black people, we granted him an equality—and perhaps a superiority—because we knew a presence was with us, one who had seen the glory.

Saints

SHEEP, GOATS AND OTHERS OF GOD'S CREATION

73

*When yellow leaves or none, or few, do hang
Upon those boughs which shake against the cold,
Bare ruined choirs, where late the sweet bird sang.*

William Shakespeare

Out of my bedroom window, I behold a bare ruined choir where late the sweet bird sang. Built down a deeply declining hillside, our new home finds my bedroom overhanging a long retaining wall which easily gives me a close up view of the downspouts of the gutters. In an almost forty-five degree angle from the roof, this sheltered spot gave a flycatcher pair the perfect spot for their nest. What busy lovers they were.

Each straw seemed to be measured, inspected and approved by each, carefully placed and replaced, edged an inch or so backwards and forward; and as the nest grew, the flycatcher hen would settle in, fan out her feathers and make suggestions about whatever moss or soft materials it would take to protect the eggs and her nestling bosom.

There was time out for courting and serenading in a shading pear tree and then onto a small outside deck where a balcony awaited Romeo and Juliet. Juliet must have been tone deaf. His "pee-tsup, pee-tsup" and "ti-ti-ti" would make a mockingbird laugh. However, the dissonance worked. Down they would flutter together onto a railing of the deck, dance around each other for a moment, and twitter some endearing sounds before the final embrace, with the shake of a few disturbed feathers. Mrs. Flycatcher would get down to nest architecture again, sending Mr. Catcher out for the finishing touches.

Sheep, Goats and Others of God's Creation

At last the nest was finished, approved, and each day an egg would be carefully laid; and as the correct number of eggs were nestled in the nest, with shining eyes of expectation, the long, tedious days of incubation began. Atop an electric pole the encouraging chirps began, and from time to time the male flycatcher's swift dart would pluck from mid-air some unsuspecting insect for a loving snack for the hen.

Since the male and female flycatchers have such similar plumage, I could not tell if they took turns on the nest; but one or the other was always there, chirping away in the cheering section. What care and devotion. Would that the Creator had endowed his fallen human family with such conjugal and parental concern.

Chicken hens take twenty-one days to hatch. I do not know about flycatchers, but I would say about the same or less. With wondrous hope in her eyes, the female had settled on her nest, awaiting with patience and promise for the new life that would be stirring beneath her. Her lover's and her genes would be passed on to sing in unknown pear trees and to rid the air of intruding stingers and zingers, all food for the birds in the hierarchy of the food chain— so wise and wonderful.

But something went awry. Sitting and sitting on her nest after too many days as the days went into weeks and finally months, the hen knew no life beneath her. Was she too old to lay sound eggs or her mate a low sperm producer? Was there some insecticide or termite spray on the nest material? What of our garden? Did the Sevin dust poison the bugs and beetles that they caught in mid-air? Did it get so cold one night that the baby flycatchers perished in their tiny shells? Did bird mites invade the nest and weaken the brooding mother as she so faithfully sat on her progeny? God only knows.

June turned into July, July turned into August, and now it is November. In August, the father flycatcher, perching on an electric wire above the pear tree, began a strange keening, an early morning low note of mourning, a dirge that was requiem. Five mornings he sang this lamentation. After that, he was seen no more. Still faithful to her calling, his mate was on her nest and she is there yet. When she died, I do not know. I never saw any signs of decay—no blow flies or change in her silhouette. I took a long pole, one I used to prop up the clothes line, and tapped the nest. There was no movement. She had given her all in faithfulness in her world of caring. There is not greater love than this. She has become to me a metaphor for the hopes and disappointments of our fallen world. I shall leave her there for the snow to enshroud, to purify, and to await the resurrection of spring when hope is made new. Then I shall bring her and her nest down.

There are those couples who long for children and they never conceive. There are those who are separated by death and their other self is gone. There are those who are poisoned by life's many mistakes and who never forgive themselves and others. There are diseases that invade our bodies and leave us questioning the "good" in the world. Worst of all is our poisoned relationships that keep us from unconditional love and true freedom. Let us learn from my flycatchers. Let us love one another.

> *Are not two sparrows sold for a penny? Yet not one of them will fall to the ground without your Father's will.*
>
> ***Matthew 10:29***

74

The best-laid schemes o'mice an'men
Gang aft a-gley

To a Mouse
Robert Burns

The poor mouse! While plowing in his wind-swept native Scotland, the poet, Robert Burns, turned up a field mouse's nest, which sent the *wee sleekit, cowerin', timorous, beastie* scampering away from its fragile refuge. The mouse's best-laid schemes for home and family had indeed gone awry.

Sheep, Goats and Others of God's Creation

This spring a pair of wrens and I also made some best-laid plans. When the first bird songs began in March with their calling and flirting in the trees, and the males looking for suitable nest sites, my pair of wrens settled on our porch where I had hung a tempting basket. What charmers they were with their exclamation-point tails. Such industry you seldom see. Soon the basket had a layer of rough straw in the bottom, then a twining of the proper sprigs of grass and vines, and a final layer of downy leaves and lichen. It was an engineering feat of a lover, lovingly fashioned for his beloved.

All the while, Mrs. Wren was popping in-and-out, inspecting each straw and commenting from the edge of the roof, seeming to suggest a better design or an alteration. The male fetched hundreds of choices—some chosen, some abandoned on the floor of the porch—but he never wavered in patience and finished his masterpiece with an arched portico, all well lined with hair from our shedding dog, Ginny, who did much basking and barking on the front porch.

Now cats we have—four of them. I began shooing them away from the front of the house, insulting them with the broom until they stared around the corner of the house with questioning eyes to see why I had become such a tyrant. The wrens were settling into nesting, and I already feared for these fledglings leaving their nest. The cats had to be trained to stay off the porch.

With wren welfare in mind, I dragged up a stepladder, fashioning a pseudo-tree and lacing limbs through the ladder's steps so the babies would have a safe place to fly out of the nest. When I knew the time for leaving the nest was at hand, front porch traffic was restricted. The parent birds were in the maple trees with encouraging words and warnings and, at the babies' first flight, frantic distress calls. Too late, too late!! Our best laid schemes were lost in a few moments.

Their two treasured, tiny wisps of life did not choose my artificial tree, but chose rather to jump to the floor. There was Ginny, our totally harmless dog, who had nothing better to do than sniff and mouth and roll the babies around until they were injured beyond all hope. Dog-murder was in my heart and tears were in my eyes.

After this tragedy there was only the wound of silence from the maple trees, a silence that echoed all the hope and love and expectations these two parent wrens had put into this new generation. I never saw them again.

Robert Burns in his poem calls himself the *mouse's poor earth-born companion and fellow mortal*. Not knowing my wrens' anguish, I could only dimly empathize with their losing two babies at one time. But we *earth-born companions and fellow mortals* are indeed predestined into the oneness of creation where no sparrow falls—or wren—*that is forgotten before God.*

God blessed his whole creation and called it good. Very good. The account of His redeeming, reclaiming, restoring, begins in Genesis and sweeps through to the final page of Revelations where the promise is made to make all things new. Our birds die, one species saves another, our mates leave us behind, our children join the baby wrens, and we desperately cling to the *ground-of-our-being*—this God who is beyond our knowing. *Our best laid schemes gang aft a-gley*, and we are tempted to despair.

But hear what Christ our Redeemer says:

> *Fear not, little flock (and that includes my wrens) for it is your Father's good pleasure to give you the kingdom. The kingdoms of the world are become the kingdom of our Lord and of his Christ, and he shall reign forever and ever.*
>
> **Luke 12, Revelation 11**

Sheep, Goats and Others of God's Creation

75

Bobby Shaftoe has a hen,
Cockle button, cockle hen
She lays eggs for gentlemen
But none for Bobby Shaftoe"

From The Real Mother Goose

Somehow Thanksgiving has me musing about hens. Why wouldn't the hen lay for Bobby Shaftoe? Why all the sayings about hens? "As scarce as hens' teeth; whistling girls and crowing hens always come to some bad end and mad as a wet hen."

Ask my mother. She was a hen expert. She knew *henology* from a setting of eggs, to the raising of the pullets (and cockerels) to the discerning of the good brood hens versus the "crowing," do-nothing kind. Woe be unto their pale combs and unruffled feathers at nesting time. Their fate was Marie Antoinette's.

Since city-bred, no chicken-exposed folks don't know the cycle of hens' activities, a history is in order. In early spring, those hens which have passed the mothering and clucking test are made new straw nests in the henhouse and allowed to lay a "setting" of eggs—about sixteen as well as I remember. There they sit, all fuss and feathers, for three long weeks, during which time there is much peeping and shuffling under the hen while she attends their emergence into this "brave new world." When the hatching is complete, the mother and chicks are given their very own coop for shelter against the elements and night-time marauders—skunks and foxes. During the day it's cluck, scratch, call, and eye the sky for hawks.

Now, if the hen gets her brood to "fry size" by the 4th of July, she has pleased the mistress of the poultry yard, as well as her household, the visiting and local preachers, and all picnic baskets. The frying victims? All cockerels—no pullets are ever fried! They are egg-layers, the on-going of the chicken genes.

These young roosters had flavor, fattened on corn, grasshoppers, worms and every form of squirming protein at their scratching places. There were never any great wads of fat, just pure essence of chicken. As the year progressed and the young roosters began to feel their testosterone and rooster fights made bloody heads in the yard, the hatchet, indeed, began to fall. The male sex was chicken and dumplings, roasted rooster and dressing, chicken pot pie, chicken salad, not to mention real, non-greasy chicken soup. We lived high on the rooster roster.

But one Thanksgiving, Mama had some crowing hens. A bad sign. Where their genetic make-up got fouled-up, only "poultrygiest" knew, but Mama said they would not be good brood hens to carry through the winter. "Off with their heads!" My aunt was visiting us and until her dying day laughed about my Thanksgiving announcement: "Guess what? We're having hen for Thanksgiving dinner. I'm so glad; I've never tasted any hen." However, I grew big and tall on the rooster diet and the bounty of my country home.

Now to answer the hen questions. Bobby Shaftoe must have been a poor chicken husbandman and didn't feed his hen. No food and there were no eggs. The hens only laid their eggs for gentlemen who treated them as a lady. This Thanksgiving I give thanks for my father and my husband who have always fed this old hen well and honored my efforts in keeping the household together. The hens have laid for these gentlemen. Keeping the household together can make one as "irritable as an old settin' hen." But I give great thanksgiving for strength to keep on keeping on in this maddening world that is our home until our days are done.

"As scarce as hens' teeth." Gentle Reader, hens have no teeth. I have never known scarcity, only abundance when it comes to food. As a nation we are so surrounded, so satiated, so inundated with food that this abundance is almost a curse. Some staple their stomachs and make them scarce like hens' teeth. This Thanksgiving, may God forgive our over-consumption in a hungry world.

And lastly the curse of the whistling girls and crowing hens! I have been both. As a child and on into adulthood and to this very hour, I whistle and sing as I do my work. Drives my family crazy! It's automatic and I sing, unaware. So far, the end hasn't been bad, and with this crowing hen, I praise the eternal love, the eternal goodness, the eternal under girding that fills me with such Thanksgiving that my praise is unutterable, a mystery of grace beyond knowing.

May you all have hen for Thanksgiving!

76

He shall feed his flock like a shepherd: he shall gather the young with his arms and carry them in his bosom, and shall gently lead those with young.

Isaiah 40

For the past two weeks the good shepherd, or in our case, the good cowherd has been gently leading his flock. The cattle on our less-than-a-thousand-hills have been his. They came to us quite unexpectedly, in crisis, starved and thirsty, with their famished calves at their sides. According to the truck driver, there had been no green pastures, no still water, no hay, no Co-op supplement—just overgrazed winter pastureland, mainly brome sedge and gravel.

An elderly and dying herdsman in Kentucky owned these cows and calves and all the winter had neglected to find them a new home. He had a mentally retarded son who supposedly was tending the cattle, but the neighbors knew this son could not do this. With all the pasture and hay gone, these friends convinced the terminally ill old farmer to let his herd of seventy cows with calves, or expecting calves, to be sold.

Knowing the same reputable cattle buyer who my husband trusts with his transactions, the neighbors called this young man for help in selling this herd for a fair price and finding them a home. But before pastures were flourishing, the buyer puzzled as to where he might send this many mother cows and calves. Some of the cows were due to deliver any moment.

This is where the good cowherd comes in, the one to feed the flock and carry the young. "Can you possibly take them?" he asked my husband. After being sick with a cold and cough for about a month, my husband had a miraculous healing, freed at last from his winter maladies. "Yes, I can do that!"

They know they are "the cattle upon a thousand hills," and the good cowherd has said, "They are mine."

Roses came back into his cheeks and out the door to check the fences and close all gates, to the barn to get the big tractor to haul hay, into the storage closet to check pneumonia medication, and to the feed store for mineral blocks, sweet-feed supplement and pour-on louse control since he had gotten a louse report. All was ready. Since my husband had sworn off cow-calf husbandry, he, no doubt, checked his delivery equipment in private. No more assisting at ungentle cow-breech births for me!

Two big cattle trucks delivered this maternity ward. Who says animals have no feeling, no sentiment, no understanding? As soon as the mother cows located their calves, who had been shipped separately, and made sure they were all right, they, with flared nostrils, seemed to sense, to smell a promise of resurrection, a release from death. Soft lowing and reassurance went from throat to throat. With their hip bones protruding through their rough coats and their empty udders swinging, they tried to nurse their babies as they filled themselves with our good hay. However, it was too late for one calf, no bigger than a poodle. It collapsed and died at its mother's side. No milk and the long truck ride had been too much.

After two days with all the feed they could eat and a thorough delousing, the herd was put out on a new pasture, fresh with spring grass and just-showing clover. Contentment filled the air. When cattle are lying down chewing their cuds, you know they are at peace with the world. The calves, still following their mothers on wobbly legs, were learning to graze in green pastures and were drinking their mother's milk to overflow.

This morning's report was good. The cattle had been gently led to a bigger pasture down by West Fork Creek, and there were three new calves this morning, born without assistance. My husband sees bones no longer protruding so boldly up the cows' backs, the hair not quite so dull, the udders are full, and the calves are beginning to play, gamboling and chasing up and down the hillsides. The good cowherd is training the herd to know his voice and come to his call when he puts feed in the troughs. To prevent pinkeye, he has anointed their heads with oil.

Surely in their bovine psyche, the mother cows know they have been deep into the valley and into the shadow of near starvation. Surely they know they are being gently led into an Easter triumph where goodness and mercy is abundant and where a banquet of sweet feed and hay has been prepared. They know they are "the cattle upon a thousand hills," and the good cowherd has said, "They are mine."

Let us rejoice with our kindred kine in the unity of creation and in the triumph that is ours.

Sheep, Goats and Others of God's Creation

77

Go into the village opposite you and immediately you will find an ass tied, and a colt with her; untie them and bring them to me. If any one says anything to you, you shall say, "The Lord has need of them," and he will send them immediately. This took place to fulfill what was spoken by the prophet, saying, "Tell the daughters of Zion, Behold, your king is coming to you, humble, and mounted on an ass, and on a colt, a foal of an ass."

Matthew 21:1-5

Go into the village opposite where on entering you will find a colt tied, on which no one has ever yet sat; untie it and bring it here. If any one asks you, "Why are you untying it?" You shall say this, "The Lord has need of it."

Luke 19

Mathew and Luke have slightly different accounts of Jesus' triumphal entry into Jerusalem—one has a mother donkey and her colt; the other the colt alone. Balaam's ass spoke, so let us hear it from the colt:

"My mother was a stubborn donkey and my father was probably some sway-backed cart horse who, no doubt, browsed along the thistly roadsides of Jerusalem by day and stole olives by night. What a pair. My mother's master tied me up, unattended and hungry, while she ran errands for the Roman ladies, who idled around in the baths all day. My education was nil. Colts had to be broken—learn to lead, know how to take the bridle, how to stay still and not buck off the rider, know the pull to left or right, and above all the command—'Whoa.' I had never even heard about—'Giddyap.' Can you believe my neglect?

Standing, tied, resting on one foot and then another, I saw two strangers approaching, and they had the nerve to untie me, saying, 'The Lord has need of you.' The Lord needs me! And no one said a word about my being taken away, no argument, just colt-napped.

Now Matthew says that my mother went along and reads as though she were needed also, but I assure you I was totally alone. For days and weeks I had dreamed about how I would rear-up, kick-up my donkey-bred heels, throw the rider off on the stony streets of Jerusalem, and bray as though I were in the promised "tin barn." But here I was untied, calm and collected, with a peace that suddenly quelled all my asinine notions.

An unknown master needed me. Who was this Master? Who could need a neglected colt—no saddle, no bridle, just a lead line? Forgetting all my determination to be the unrideable colt, I followed without question into a great multitude of this Master's disciples who threw their garments onto me and placed the man Jesus on my back. The descent from the Mount of Olives went wild. Again garments came off the great gathering, making a red carpet for Jesus and me; and others on our way spread leafy branches which they had cut from the fields, all the while shouting and praising God.

My donkey ears were used to loud noises but these were different. "Hosanna, blessed is he who comes in the name of the Lord. Hosanna in the highest!" On my untried back rode a king totally unlike any haughty Roman royalty that I had ever seen. His royalty was in his humility, and I could feel through the saddle garments that his love and respect included us poor street animals. I learned later that his Father counted all of creation good and that nothing was outcast, no half-breed colts or sons-of-donkeys.

Via the Roman grapevine, my mother heard that some of these Hosanna people had given up on this Jesus whom they would make an earthly king. Their Hosannas became 'Crucify him.' I thought that we untrained colts were devious, but can you believe this 180 degree turn-around? As for me, I was never the same after our triumphal ride together. I had been chosen to bear on my back the King of Kings; the Lord of Lords. Who would ever believe my report?"

I believe his report and I believe the colt knows us to this very hour. We are a mixture of "Hosannas" and "Crucify Him." We praise and throw down our garments before our King, but in the next breath curse our neighbors and forget that they are included in God's prodigal love. When will we ever learn? May we ride the chosen colt this Easter and let him show us the importance of taking the bridle, of bearing our precious loads, of following with faith without too many questions, ignoring the confusion and shouts along our way, and, at last, knowing the difference between "giddyap" and "whoa."

78

And if any soul sin through ignorance, then he shall bring a she-goat of the first year for a sin offering.

Ezekiel 34-17

How many she goats would it take to blot out our sins of ignorance! My husband and I have already tried a half dozen. We didn't sacrifice and sprinkle any goat blood, but left ourselves in ignorance, sins unexpiated. However, we did become wiser to goats' superior knowledge of good and evil, and my goat cursing expletives increased exponentially.

As you know, my husband was a seafaring man during World War II, and for some time afterwards, leaving me behind to cope with children, crops, chickens, chiggers, cockleburs, crabgrass, and every other portion of Adam's curse. Cocklebur Heaven was the name given our plantation with these stickers thriving in the front yard, snagging our stockings and threatening our bare feet.

One spring when the young mariner was at home for a long stay, we decided to make war on the weeds and burrs in the lots around the stable and pond. A flash of brilliance came—"Goats, yes, goats. They will eat anything, keep those lots better than a Yazoo mower, and be pleasant company, gamboling about and bleating Pan-like melodies through the burrs and nettles. When they will have finished their eating duties, Eden will be somewhat restored and we will bask on the lawn." Ignorance is indeed bliss.

At my husband's order, Mr. Edgar Rye, pen hooker and experienced trader in most any sort of flesh—cloven-hoofed or otherwise—delivered in his nose-clearing truck our environmentally-safe weed control. We were the proud owners of six nanny goats. A billy goat was left out because we had been warned of too much goat romance that would take the nannies' minds off their duties. Here began our education into goat mores and preferences, and our ignorance was soon to understand why that she-goat needed to be sacrificed for a sin offering—especially the one of wrath.

The first few days the goats were recluses, hiding in their new home. You could see a few tall horse weeds waving and get a glimpse of them passing by the woven wire fence that was their boundary. But why weren't the weeds coming down and new vistas opening in the barn lot? Remember, "Goats will eat anything." Our ignorance of goat menus was complete. Unlike cattle, goats are browsers, nibbling at the leaves and tips of bushes, climbing into honeysuckle vines, seeking out often undesirable plants that other animals won't eat. God in his wisdom created goats for bushes and briars in arid places where other animals could not survive. Rather than eating our succulent grass and weeds in the lots, they preferred pastures that prickled. They knew in their goat digestion good from evil.

My goats waited to get aggressive about their favorite foods until my husband's departure and they had eaten all the sassafras bushes. They were adorned with thin curly horns arched back from their brows; and they began sticking their heads through the woven wire fence, either out of curiosity or craving for brush. When they put their heads through the fence, they were caught. There was no way out. You know who was the goat-releaser! You cannot imagine the strength of a pilloried she-goat. I had to pull their heads forward, align their ridged horns backward, and push their heads through the woven wire.

Sheep, Goats and Others of God's Creation

Have you ever looked a goat in the eyes? They have these almost-human yellow eyes and while you are freeing them, they accuse you in such bleating anguish as though you were Judas Iscariot. I thought they would learn about the fence but, NO, they didn't. First thing every morning, I ran the fence to set the captives free and last thing every night, all of which made me decide the goats were bored and wanted to see what was going on beyond their world. Maybe we should have gotten that billy goat after all.

After some weeks of this duty and to keep me from sacrificing a she-goat for my sins of ire and ignorance, I called Mr. Rye who came and took our scapegoats to another wilderness, leaving our weeds intact and my language expanded.

This recounting of the goats' sojourn set me mulling and musing about our sins through ignorance. I look back down the years and am aware of sins that were plainly from not knowing, from ignorance. As a child and a young person, I was not aware of the indignities that we did to other persons—looking down on them because of their poverty or race. Then there were my unrecognized sins of worshipping false gods—the gods of power and position, craving to be identified with these gods. The sin of self-righteousness had me in its thralls, and I did not know that I could not make myself good. I was ignorant of Grace. As I have grown old, I have sacrificed many she-goats and have confessed my sins through ignorance—and am still confessing them. I was blind but now I am seeing much more clearly. Thanks be to God and she goats.

Sheep, Goats and Others of God's Creation

79

All things bright and beautiful
All creatures great and small
All things wise and wonderful
The Lord God made them all.

Cecil Frances Alexander

Grandchildren and grand dogs are wonders. When our older son and his wife had their only child, a daughter, they couldn't tend her and Tess, their loud mouthed Schnauzer. Thus I had a grand dog. This past Christmas our daughter went for five weeks to France to be with her two sons. You guessed it. I have a grand cat.

His name is "Minou" which is French for kitty cat. What a wonder he is! Our dear friend, Hazel Irwin, who is a champion of all stray cats, told me of a most handsome "Russian Blue" that either strayed or had been dropped in their community and had become her and her neighbors' responsibility. Since they were all well catted, Hazel wanted this gorgeous purr-ball to have a permanent home, a place to truly exhibit his beauty, brains, and infinite store of loving and purring.

Our daughter Emily to the rescue. She had returned to the States after 22 years in Paris, where she lived until her two grown sons were out of the nest. Her farm roots wanted to be planted back home, which found her moving into a shamble of a farm house near Trenton, Kentucky. Her first need for her household: a cat. I do believe in the communion of saints, the coincidentals of circumstances, the majestic movement of the lover of all creatures great and small.

Hazel had Emily's Minou. She had him in an animal carrier but there was no need because he purred and loved us all the way from Hazel's home on Mobley Road in Montgomery County to Tutt Road in Todd County, Kentucky. Not one complaining meow or terrified scratching came from him. He knew all was well. Emily calls Minou her third son. She says he understands anything she says. On cold days, she asks him if he wants to stay in while she is away or does he want out. He loves the outdoors. She says he thinks a few moments and considers the weather before he makes up his mind. He curls in this chair as refusal or springs for the door for his outdoor haunts. When Emily returns from her work, she starts blowing her horn at the beginning of a long drive to the house, and wherever Minou is, they greet for much purring and mutual loving.

Who says animals don't have emotions? They grieve and despair. Emily went back to France for over a month to be with her sons for Christmas, and you know who got to keep her cat. Knowing absolute freedom on the Trenton farm, Minou had to live in our basement and the upstairs. We are close to the street on Chapel Hill Road and the one time I let him out, he went immediately to the very center stripe and ran down the road. I finally rescued him and into prison he went for the rest of his stay. I'm sure he was headed back to Trenton. From door to door, window to window, upstairs and downstairs, "Oh, for a way out." We were most careful opening doors lest he run past us. After about ten days, he gave up hope, as I am sure people in prison do. He sat on the back of the couch looking out or curled up somewhere asleep. He slept and ate and gained weight. His joy of living had gone. He loved me but I wasn't Emily. Grief was in his eyes and gloss was gone from his fur. Hope was gone.

Now for the happy ending. Minou's disbelief at the sight of his beloved mistress was a rejoicing to behold. They had a special way of play with much rolling and tumbling and fur scratching and talking. There is a special utterance in Minou's throat when he is happy. There was no need for a cage to go home. Minou watched, propped at the front seat's window for each curve in the road and each familiar sight. When they rounded the corner at Mrs. Haley's

How did Tess our Schnauzer know when Sunday came around and her bath was due?

house, his good friend, Minou knew he was home. Bounding out of the car, he disappeared into the cold night to check out the frog pond, the mice in the abandoned chicken house, and the sleeping lizards hiding under the porch. The next day was sleep, sleep, delicious sleep in his chair by the fire. Paradise lost; paradise regained.

Animals have a dimension beyond our human understanding. How do they know when it's going to storm? Ask our dog Jennie. How did Tess our Schnauzer know when Sunday came around and her bath was due? How did Harry, our Doberman, know when Jack was going to the back of the farm or into town? If town, he stayed in the yard; if back of the farm, he was at the proper gate.

Look out your window, look into the skies, look at your kitty cat. Aren't all things bright and beautiful? There is wisdom and wonder in creation, a marvel of unfathomable majesty and mystery too transcendent for our infant senses that seldom rise above our confused caps. "God does not regard any who are wise in their own conceit," and he gives understanding to creatures great and small, which certainly includes my grand dog and my grand cat.

80

Many bulls have compassed me; bulls of Bashan have beset me round.
Psalm 22

I have known personally quite a few bulls. When I was a child, Daddy warned me against Old Scamp, a dirty-yellow Jersey with keen horns and a mean, dirt-pawing temper. "Never trust a bull," he told us children as he cracked Scamp around the ears with a tobacco stick. Neighbors brought to our barnyard lowing cows, tugging at their halters, because we had a "male" or more genteelly—"a gentleman cow." One of my childhood mysteries was being banished to the house as my father introduced Scamp to his latest captive conquest.

Sheep, Goats and Others of God's Creation

When we began farming and my husband had brood cows, I was introduced to shorthorn bulls, no-horn bulls, Angus, Hereford, and various exotic blends as we bred for length and breadth and bone and on-and-on for attributes to increase the nation's cholesterol. These bulls did not compass me round because they free-roamed among the herd and beset the latest heifer, hoping to find romance on the range. However, Daddy's words of warning stayed with me through the years until, in my old age, I got at ease and trusting of bulls. As a result, a strong bull of Bashan almost bashed me.

We got a new neighbor down Pollard Road who had dreams of being a cattleman after his retirement from the army. Off to the market he goes and came home with twenty cows and a two-thousand-pound Angus bull. From the very start Angus had no idea of staying at home—probably the reason he was on the market—and he always made a dash for our place. Why, I don't know. We only had steers, which, City Reader, are bulls who have had an operation. We would herd him home, his owner patched the fence, Angus promptly flattened it again, and back he came for his visit. Our new game for the fall season was *Pen the Bull*.

On my way to the mailbox one Saturday morning, I saw Angus eyeing our steers and eating honeysuckle in the fencerow. "Here we go again." I called my husband and we started our usual routine of getting this philanderer down the fence to a holding pen and then calling our neighbor to help us get him home. This morning, Angus wasn't his usual docile self. He seemed to resent this intrusion into his honeysuckle and honey-filled ideas. He did a haughty snort, turned on his massive round steaks, bounded a ditch, lowered his head, and charged me! And I had no cape, only a scream that must have awakened the heavenly host of guardian angels because just as his massive head was on a beeline collision course with my vitals, he veered to my left. I could feel his wind rush by.

To quote David again after his encounter with the bulls of Bashan, "I am poured out like water, and all my bones are out of joint; my heart is like wax; it is melted in the midst of my bowels...and my tongue cleaveth to my jaws." And if I might be so bold as to add a verse to Psalm 22: "I clingeth to a fence post and Jello doest overcome my extremities." Too late the warning, "Never trust a bull."

After my heart glued back together and my knees firmed up, I began to mull and muse this chronicle of bull. One of the prayers of my seventy-two years is the one that all persons my age must pray: "Please, Lord, may I not be a burden in my last years. Please, Lord, let my brain outlast my body. Please, Lord, no nursing home for me. Let a rock fall on me—anything." And here I just blew the perfect answer to my prayer and a newsworthy one at that. No ho-hum dying in bed, but headlines in the paper: "Bull Overcomes Local Cowgirl." Rather than accepting this clear answer to my prayers and offering the neighborhood some notoriety, I scream and implore heavenly intervention, hastily calling out my guardian angel who must think me totally ambivalent about my requests. Surely I was saved for some yet unknown purpose—maybe to reflect further and separate the transitory from the transcendent.

After Angus and Christmas and New Year, I took stock: Surely it's not how big my bank account is, or my house, or my car, my wardrobe, or my diamond ring. Such earthly matters pale into unimportance as I muse over my years. It is how big the capacity of my heart has become in treasuring those immeasurable gifts that are mine: children and grandchildren, a good husband, an ever-growing circle of friends, and finally, the greatest gift of all—the sure foundation that I am accepted and cherished, here and now and always, by a loving God who has saved me from both the literal and the figurative bulls of Bashan and has included me in being His presence in the world. What glorious knowledge.

> *"I will disclose thy name unto my brethren: in the midst of the congregation will I praise thee."*
>
> **Psalm 22:22**

P.S. Our neighbor sold Angus the week of this episode. Thanks be to God!

81

You shall know the truth, and truth shall make you free.

John 8:32

My husband had a friend who was a breeder of "fighin" chickens. Now a royal highness rooster had to be put out on a "walk" with some hens so he could preen his glorious tail feathers, strut around the hens with inviting chortles for worms—which he promptly guzzled down—and brag of his crowing ability from midnight until well after sunrise. This was the cock-of-the-walk, the essence of manly chicken testosterone.

With some misgivings from me since my husband was sailing away to foreign climes, the chickens were put under my wing. Now old Dominique (Southern pronunciation—Dominecker) and Rhode Island Red roosters I know, ones you could shoo off the front porch or out of the flower beds with a broom. They were reasonable roosters, turned tail and went out into the back yard to scratch and dust themselves.

Now this sleek fighting machine with his clicking spurs was another story. He feared neither broom nor beast. His Highness had Wolfgang, our waggy dog, soon his vassal that lost his front yard holdings and became a watchdog, watching mainly for that mean rooster. The gamecock was reputed by his owner to be worth at least a thousand dollars with his blood line going back to the Spanish Inquisition or some other tortuous period. For a breeding rooster, his genes were to produce winners in the states where cock fights were legal, illegal, permitted, or banned. With the money right, the local sheriffs knew which, when and where.

Into my front yard with his harem in tow, this cock-of-the-walk took over my flower beds. There was not enough wire, brush or broom to keep him from somehow getting under the fence into the loose dirt, where he scratched and dusted himself, all the while calling the ladies to join him in some choice morsel, which he promptly ate.

Those hens were pushovers for fine feathers.

I was irate. I had spaded and sweated and here this interloper was desecrating my sweat. Out came the broom which caused some sassy sidesteps, some chortles, an impressive strut, ending in a victorious "cock-a-doodle-do." Momentarily, he would retreat, but by the time I got back in the house, the same scene. I determined to cock his doodle do.

"That cock-sure feather duster is afraid of nothing! Wonder how he would respond to hot lead?" I found a rifle I could handle with a loud reverberation, and I would fire it either under his feet or just over the top of his head to see if a rifle blast would scare him. I took dead aim right above his head as he was pecking away at my blossoms, and just as I pulled the trigger, he raised his head. Right through his eyeballs! I had murdered the thousand-dollar rooster.

"My, my, what to do?" Charles, our older son, was about 3 years old and witnessed the execution. What could I tell the owner and my husband about the disappearance of this noble bloodline? As Sir Walter Scott wrote: "We must practice to deceive." Charles and I took this gold-plated braggart, who would have made fine dumplings, down a steep bluff behind our house and flung him where no mortal eye would see. What "tangled web" of deception could I weave? I had to coach Charles. Was I going to teach my child to lie? "When your daddy comes home, don't say anything about the rooster. Remember, just be quiet. Now don't forget." Then I told him that when his daddy asked about this prize-winner, I would remind him, "remember the pack of wild dogs, and there have been reports of coyotes in the area." No direct lie in this line.

At length Daddy came home from the sea. As he came down the steps from the plane, what was the first greeting from our son? "Daddy, Mama shot your rooster." "Out of the mouths of babes…"

This has been one of the laughable stories in our family, and I look back on it and wonder why I was so afraid of the bare truth. I was not mature enough to know that only truth works, that facing it is the beginning of our freedom, the path to being set free.

The egotistical rooster personifies the bravado and facades that we create to hide behind. In each of us is that dark, hidden tangle of old angers, jealousies, guilts-that-I-could-never-confess-to-anyone-places all too painful to face. But these dark closets of our soul will out. We see our world through their shadow. We judge in others what we most dislike in ourselves.

We need to kill some roosters. It is only when we allow the truth to shine into our darkness and we face and confess our judgments that we start to become real and free. Arrogance I dislike because I know my arrogance of spirit, lies I dislike because I know all the deceptions within me, gossip I hate because I know how I love to hear it—it makes me somehow feel superior. Where is the real me? When shall I be set free?

Blessed are the rooster-shooters, for theirs is the Kingdom of Truth.

82

I shall not ask Jean Jacques Rousseau, if birds confabulate or no.

William Cowper

Mama didn't have to ask Jean Jacques Rousseau. Come spring, she knew birds confabulated. With this knowledge in mind, and the rooster's comb red and the hens cackling, she began her plans to populate the poultry yard. New nests were a must, chicken-mite dust was sprinkled among the fresh straw, and my poor brother had to sanitize the roost poles, hauling a winter's worth of chicken manure to the garden.

Sheep, Goats and Others of God's Creation

After many springs of chickens only, Mama decided to diversify. Why not some larger fowl? Maybe some turkeys to swell her paltry poultry coffers around Thanksgiving and Christmas?

Kind fortune was already with her because she knew Fanny Tyler, our wash lady who lived about three farms away, had a lone, mature and living turkey gobbler that she had been trying to find a home. Fanny did not bring Tom Turkey to our house under any false pretenses, laying out in advance his bird-brained idiosyncrasies.

"Miss Maude, this turkey think he's folks. He so lonesome he hang around the door all day, just waitin' for me to come out so he can strut and dance around my feets. He's in love with my shoes. When I sets down to rest, he come and perch on my feets and act like he makin' love. I guess 'cause he ain't never seen no turkey hens."

Mama knew the remedy for Tom's needs. Nine last-season's turkey pullets, ready for mating and setting, were procured at some extravagant price, perhaps 50 cents each and were placed in a pen with Tom. At last, Tom would have his frustrations eased and he would join the ornithological world and forget his Fanny-feet-fetish.

The best laid plans of Mamas and turkeys "gang aft a-gley." All day long Tom paced the fence toward the house and when Mama or some other female showed herself, he would go into a flurry of strutting and dancing, rather like a Spanish dancer mad at the floor. The turkey hens didn't get a feather raised for them. This went on for days and finally, in desperation, Mama turned her turkey project out to graze the orchard and build their nests in some private place. As for Tom, he turkey-trotted to the back door if we were in the kitchen or to the front door if we were cooling on the porch.

There was no respite from his advances and he knew well the sex of his choice. He loved all women and despised all men. A skirt came into the yard, and she was met with such gobbling and preening as to sicken a gigolo. But let a pair of pants arrive, and they were met with such vicious darting and flogging as to send them up a tree or back into their car. Even though my brother was always there, Tom never forgave him for being a male and would hide in the hydrangea bush by the back door, waiting for my brother to appear so he could fly up at his head, dig in his spurs and flog him all the way down.

This hatred was mutual. Once when my brother was dressed in new clothes, ready to go out on a date, Tom sneaked up on his backside and flogged him through a barbed wire fence, tearing his new pants as well as relieving him of some skin. This was too much. Being a football player and knowing the drop kick, my brother, new clothes and all, ran Tom down, wrestled him to the ground, held his sex-starved feet, and kicked him until he was silly; and, as a finality, drop-kicked him over a fence.

We thought perhaps this reverse flogging would be the end of Tom, but like the Phoenix, he rose from his ashes more bitter and more determined to wreak havoc on all human males and to make love to all female feet who graced our front porch. Long ago the pale turkey hens had ceased to peep into the front yard to see this object of their disaffection. The turkey project had turned into a real "turkey."

During the late summer and fall, chicken "pen hookers" came through the community with coops on the back of their jalopies and offered to buy fryers and hens in the yard. Mama saw her opportunity. Not only would she sell some chickens, but she had this fine gobbler in the front yard ready for someone's Thanksgiving dinner.

"Would you be interested in a fine turkey at a reasonable price?"

For two dollars, Tom, surrounded by every vengeful male nearby, was chased through orchard, through horseweeds and bull nettles, down the briar-filled lane behind the hog lot, and at last, trussed with twine string and stuffed into a burlap bag. My brother's one

Sheep, Goats and Others of God's Creation

remark at Tom's departure—"Whoever gets that turkey for Thanksgiving won't get a fork in the gravy." We knew for sure what confabulate meant and for some summers we watched our feet while sitting on the front porch.

In the world of birds—geese and cranes in particular—attachments are made to their first caretaker; and if, by chance their natural mother is not there for them, they attach themselves to their adoptive parents and slavishly follow them. Tom Turkey knew only Fanny as parent and loved only her kind.

The moral of this turkey tale must be about our inordinate bondings, some made in the dim shadows of our childhood that follow us all our days. Often they can be traced to our parents or other authority figures who make an imprimatur that holds us in its iron mold. These hang-ups can be legion: "Never waste money; you must watch every penny. Don't marry someone beneath you. Remember, there are germs on every doorknob. You must be a lawyer like your father..." And on and on.

Our bird brains and foolish fetishes are liberated when we surrender our very being, our innermost spirit, to a maturity of love that comes to us as we seek to find ourselves and knock to let ourselves be opened. Our liberty is in the freedom of this love that is God.

> *Therefore let us lay aside every weight and sin which clings so closely and let us run with perseverance the race that is set before us...*
>
> ***Hebrews 12***

83

Consider the lilies of the field, how they grow; they neither toil nor spin; yet I tell you, even Solomon in all his glory was not arrayed like one of these.

Matthew 7

As the Easter parade approached Kirkwood with its demands for new clothes, we began to "toil and spin." My sister, ever the fashion plate, searched the pages of the Vogue pattern book for the latest in Paris fashion, and with her innate dexterity with needle and thread came up with some lily-rivaling creations. Simplicity pattern book was congruent with my talents, since I had a red sewing thumb which called forth much seam ripping and unarticulated bad language.

A new hat for Easter was a must. Our mother was an original along the millinery line, resurrecting straw hats long relegated to the attic shelves with drooping brims and discouraged blossoms. They were brought forth, steamed, starched, pressed, and at last arrayed with a wide choice of silk flowers, feathers, ribbons, and laces, all chosen from a bag of frou-frou of historic significance. If there were not enough period pieces in the bag, Mama went to either McNeal and Edwards or Pearsons' millinery departments where she could find the latest whimsy for stopping the Easter Parade.

One Easter for my sister she fashioned a white cartwheel hat with a lone pink cabbage rose that must have been eight inches across. For me, it was multiple white poppies that floated on a sea of green veiling, interlaced with black ribbon. How elegant we felt! To be honest, we were all decked out in our Easter regalia for one purpose: to be looked at and admired. But just as this time of self-absorption into the adorning of the flesh came an interspersion, a lesson we needed to learn—the lesson of Beulah.

This teacher, Beulah, was my brother's high-bred Irish setter. "Upsetter" would have been a better name. She was ordered out of Iowa and came to us by rail, bounded out of her cage and promptly took over the household. My mother's house, and particularly her bed, were sacrosanct—but not to Beulah. Right away she chose our mother's bed for her private boudoir. On the white bedspread, she dragged old shoes, corn cobs, and assorted smelly objects which caused a great flurry of Beulah-banishment. As if by magic, she was somehow in again, on the bed, with an ever-increasing collection of grisly objects, chosen for their aromatic and long-lasting chewing qualities.

On the Easter Sunday of the cabbage rose and poppy hats, Beulah reached her apogee. She was bred to appreciate feathers and fluttery creatures like quail in hunting season, and she performed true to breeding. When we got home from church, we took off our hats and placed them—where?—on Mama's bed, of course. In the meantime, there was Easter dinner going on in the kitchen and dining room and we forgot all about Beulah. When dinner was finished and we came back into our mother's room, there Beulah, in all her glory, had flowers and feathers and other frou-frou all around her mouth, straw wildly strewn over the entire bed, and several abandoned pigs' bones arranged on the starched pillow cases.

When we took in this scene, we somehow had the grace to laugh. We laughed, we whooped, tears ran down our faces, all of which unsettled Beulah and she, tuck-tailed, asked to go outside to recover her composure. Unknown to her, she had provided us with a family story that yet survives; and with the destruction of our hats, she brought into focus a critical look at our shallow pretensions and the folly of Easter hats. "Even Solomon in all his glory was not arrayed like one of these." One lily of the field far outshone all our toiling and spinning. From that day I began to hear Isaiah's words anew—"why do you spend your money and your labor for that which does not satisfy?"

Some criticize the casual and unpretentious dress of the current Easter parade. Gone are the hats and gloves and new outfits with corsages. I say, "Thank you, Beulah; we don't have to do that anymore!" Christ in his Sermon on the Mount told us, long before Beulah, that we needed food and clothes, all these things and it was

Sheep, Goats and Others of God's Creation

the Father's good pleasure to give us all we needed. But we are to seek first his kingdom and his righteousness and, if we do that, all else will fall into place.

At this Easter season, we are given all things—the assurance of forgiveness for all our mess-ups, the under girding of a love which will not let us go even though we forget such love, and at the end, the grace to abandon our toiling and spinning to the risen Christ who will make us new, arrayed with beauty unimaginable. We shall be lilies of his field, and Beulah shall bound among us. Easter joy and love to all!

84

All things bright and beautiful,
All creatures great and small,
All things wise and wonderful
The Lord God made them all

The furry little kitties
With claws as sharp as steel,
He gave them jungle passion
To create as they will.

Cecil Frances Alexander and COM

For years I have watched nature on PBS and always, but always, you are allowed an intimate scene of mating, over-sexed monkeys, hippos oozing in the mud, whales wallowing in amorous embraces, giraffes weaving on stilts to the object of their affection, elephants following patiently for the right moment, and birds which bill and entwine their necks for hours, politely in love. But what of feline romance? Is there no camera fast enough to catch the action?

I have been awakened in the night to cat screams as they whirled round and round, threatening the foundation of the house. There seems to be absolutely no cooperation on the female's part. Her virtue has to be snatched away, violently and vocally, as she is held by the nape of the neck in the tom's death-grip jaws. This I have never seen on PBS—only heard it, eerily in the night; but I have an eyewitness account.

My brother suffered a broken ankle from a skateboard fall. Confined to the couch with his cast propped on the coffee table, he languished, away from work, complaining bitterly of immobility, boredom, and an unscratchable itch deep inside his plaster, all the while enslaving his nursemaid wife. Oh, for some respite from this tedium!

One evening, Johnny, their new cat, presumed to be a male, was sleeping underneath my brother's outstretched leg while he snoozed on the couch. Under their hillside home was their first floor basement with a long stair leading up to the main floor into the den. Rule No.1: Keep the basement door closed at all times to keep out chipmunks, thieves, snakes, but they forgot tomcats.

Johnny, who should have been Johnnie, was in heat and her delicious aromas, no doubt, were perfuming all the northeast Atlanta. With no warning, just an earth-moving scream, Old Tom grabbed Johnnie by her innocent neck and underneath my brother's immobility began the rape of Johnnie's nine lives. My brother recalls the details, which have grown better through the years; from beneath his leg, the coupling proceeded up the curtains, in the den, down a long hall, into two bedrooms, all the while spraying and perfuming the new bedspreads and wallpaper with all the excreted passions of primordial procreation. My brother vowed that a 7-pound cat held 10 pounds of love potions.

Hopping on one leg and with crutch in hand, he tried in vain to stop this carnage and finally got it out of the kitchen onto the carport. My brother's wife had to finish the report of this cat orgy: Way into the night she was stripping beds, wiping down walls, throwing carpets out into the yards, all the while taking out her fury on my brother's helplessness.

Where can I find a moral for this month's musings? Keep your basement door closed; check your cat's sex? Or marvel at the

Sheep, Goats and Others of God's Creation

diversity and continuing complexity of God's creation? I shall choose the latter for God said it was "good." He goes before us with his fecundity and originality, his boundless bounty and love beyond knowing. Some Biblical translations read—"In the beginning, God began creating the heavens and the earth." Can we earthlings, bound to Genesis, consider that we are emerging, changing, growing and becoming more complex with God going before us, leading us into some new Promised land, out of encrusted patterns into a higher level of creation? Forget John Calvin and predestination! We have emerged from Ice man to Mozart, from caves to the Taj Mahal, from notches on sticks to computers, from kites to Mars. Are we not sustained within the divine creator "in whom we live and move and have our being" and who draws us out of our deserts of dried assumptions and ultimately out of ourselves into a higher realm of becoming?

Tom Kitty is still in the grab-them-by-the-hair stage and, like many of us, has not emerged from cave man's trust in power. Let us know the more excellent way—Tenderness is strength and "strength is made perfect in weakness." What a radical emergence from St. Paul.

Emerge us, Ground of our Being, to your higher ground where the greatest among us loves his enemies, feeds them, and is servant to all.

UNORTHODOXY AND QUESTIONABLE THEOLOGY

85

I can will what is right, but I cannot do it. For I do not do the good I want, but the will I do not want is what I do.

St. Paul in Romans 7

St. Paul, we need to join your club. The New Year with its resolutions is here so what shall we do? Ah, ha! The Ten Commandments; and my daddy was most grateful they didn't have a "shalt not" about chewing tobacco.

Ten Commandments 101. Let's post them, carve them, emblazon them in our church yards, at the courthouse, at the Salvation Army, The Black Horse Pub, over our kitchen sinks, and as reading material in private places. The Law will get us right.

The first and great commandment, we know well. "You shall have no other gods before me." Maybe this won't be as easy as I thought. Whatever is foremost in my heart and mind is my god. Could it be "me, myself, and I?" You are a jealous God, so you want my body, soul, mind, and strength and where does that leave me whose body and mind demand glorification, beautification, and much repair work? You are too jealous. Bad grade on First Commandment.

Now to the second, the one about graven images. We confess we have Jesuses, bloody and beaten on the cross; sainted Marys in stained glass; and masterpieces, both painted and carved, all over Christendom. As for present day graven images, we worship at the sight of sleek cars, dazzling diamonds, dream houses, and yes, the image of St. Pigskin in the Field. Moses' course? Maybe a C-.

"You shall not take the name of the Lord your God in vain"—the third commandment. Now Mama allowed no taking of the Lord's name in vain. No "goshes, gollys, dad-burns, dog gones, good Lords, Lord have mercy" and certainly never, no-never, any G-D---s. We had never heard the f--- word. Mama called this "strong language." Too, she suspicioned some Kirkwood Church prayers as taking The Lord's name in vain. "Their prayers never got above their coattails." Maybe a passing grade on this one.

"Remember the Sabbath day to keep it holy." As a child at the Kirk-in-the-Woods, we kept the Sabbath as holy as was required of us: no card playing, no movie going, no shopping since there were no places to shop. Moses, we must confess our Sabbath-keeping has gone to the dogs of consumerism and our insatiable need for entertainment. This Sunday past, I desecrated this holy day to the wholly unholy by going to see *Borat*, a movie my mama would have fled at the first frame. It was a scatological and perverted satire of our present day culture at its worst. I enlarged my vocabulary but flunked syntax appreciation. Zero on Sabbath keeping.

With the promise of long days in the land, Moses carved into his stones to "Honor thy father and mother." I tried. However, I drag old guilts out of my guilt attic which say I didn't do this honoring too well. At the end of my mother's life, which was at ninety-five, I had a testing-time honoring her. She lived with me, and as her caretaker, she took her frustrations out on me—poor sweet, good little me! Have pity, Moses. Let me pass this one.

Here come the "shall nots"—kill, commit adultery, steal, bear false witness, and covet. This is the final exam and thanks be to God that Christ's teaching updates Moses'. Hating one's brother is like killing him and you will be brought to judgment. How many notches on my hate gun? Lusting in your heart is adultery. How many times at fourteen did I commit adultery with Nelson Eddy, a long-ago movie idol who sang like Israfel. Who hasn't stolen—maybe someone's good name—and lied? Show me one person and I'll eat the limestone ten commandments on the grounds of Kenwood Baptist Church.

At my age, I'm almost too old to covet? However, I do covet the glorious music of Anne Glass and Lisa Bishop; the brains of Richard Gildrie and Ed Irwin; and the drop-dead beauty of Louisa Conroy. But back to the mundane word: my house is just right after fifty-four years; I don't covet anyone's husband because my husband is my maid-servant; and how could I ever covet my neighbor's ox or his ass? His ox might gore me and I wouldn't know what to do with his ass. This is not "strong language." See Exodus 20. Incomplete on this one.

What shall St. Paul and I do with our failing grades? Hear what he says: "Who will deliver me from this body of death?...Thanks be to God through Jesus Christ our Lord...There is therefore no condemnation for those who are in Christ Jesus. For the law of the spirit of life in Christ has set me free from the law of sin and death."

His law is our new commandment. "Let us love one another." This love fulfills all the laws and prophesies. Moses, shut your grade book! The forgiveness and acceptance we know in Christ makes us all A+.

A blessed 2007 and my love to y'all all, which is the plural of y'all.

86

And Peter opened his mouth and said: "truly I perceive that God shows no partiality, but in every nation anyone who fears him and does what is right is acceptable to him.

Acts 10

There is nothing like adult children to get us old folks out of our dull doldrums. Our only daughter, Emily, is a prime example of mama-moving. Having lived in Paris some twenty-two years and being near a Greek Orthodox Church, she with some regularity

Unorthodoxy and Questionable Theology

would go to their mass to experience this unique service of sights, sounds, smells and bells, all foreign to our Southern, Protestant background.

"Mama, have you ever been to a Greek Orthodox Church? We must go for your ecumenical spirit to be broadened." And I am all for that.

Away we go three Sundays past to the Holy Trinity Greek Orthodox Church at 4905 Franklin Pike, Nashville, where I stepped into a world far beyond my ken. It was the fifth Sunday from Pascha—Sunday of the Samaritan woman, who is named Saint Photing. Going to my dictionary, I found this "Pascha" is the Greek word for Passover and also Easter. Abraham Lincoln read the dictionary. So should I.

With icons' accusing eyes following me and the twelve apostles judging from the high altar, we were fumigated time and again with great flourishes of swinging incense that would have cleared Trinity's pews in a few minutes. All this cleaning was accompanied by a never-ending liturgy, sung in the "fourth tone", all strange to my song-book ears. There was a low monotone bass line, rather like a one-tone bullfrog, never ending, which supported about five notes up and down some mode unknown to me. It was ad infinitum-five men only, droning the liturgy. My ignorance was complete.

The congregation seemed to be only spectators, coming and going throughout the two hour service. They kissed various venerated objects up and down the aisles, kissed the priest's ring, but were absolutely silent. I got a disapproving stare when I asked Emily a question about where we were in the prayer book, much of it written in Greek.

Now to the priest himself. He was a Greek god, an Adonis. His robes would pale our bishop's regalia into work clothes. His vestments were adorned with precious stones, golden bangles, accompanied by bejeweled books and great circled standards whose symbolism was more ignorance added to my great

Unorthodoxy and Questionable Theology

collection. To gild this Adonis more, he had a singing voice worthy of the Met, and he blessed and "incensed" us over and over with stentorian vocals, all in Greek.

There was a mystery about this man. He had been an Episcopalian and had been in Nashville before; but this priest was leaving as of this writing, called to New York City by Archbishop Demetrios to be the Archdiocese's Director of Ecumenical and Interfaith Relations. At the coffee hour not being one afraid to ask questions, I asked him if he were called to be the ecumenical and interfaith person, how could he limit the baptized Christians in his midst away from Christ's table. Too, I asked him WHY he left the Episcopal Church. He gave me "double speak" on both questions. He must have thought "fools rush in", and I forgave him because he was so "easy on my eyes."

Leaving one so unbelievably handsome in Nashville and coming home to one so unbelievably honest and good on the corner of Cumberland Drive and Crossland Avenue, we tell you of the Reverend Mr. James Mackens. He is the pastor of the Church of God of Prophecy at Cumberland Furnace. He and Emily have mutual interest: antiques, chair repair, salvaged junk, six-dollar per yard fabric of every description, and piles of mysterious treasures waiting to be discovered. Added to his possessions, Mr. Mackens is master of upholstery and furniture repair—some fifty years' plus experience. He is generous with his knowledge, giving Emily lessons on "how to" and what is good and no good, all the while loving our immortal souls and inviting us to his church.

We went for his birthday celebration. This included dinner-on-the-grounds, imported Southern gospel musicians from Kentucky, and preaching by one of Mr. Machens' sons whose focus was on fatherhood, including God, Abraham, and his own father. There were many "Praise the Lords" and "Amens" with a sweet spirit flowing through this gathering of God's people. Unlike our Greek Orthodox priest, Mr. Mackens is no Adonis, but he has a handsomeness of spirit and a humility of spirit that shines through his face and you forget flaws in his physique which show his many years of bending to resurrect chairs, long abandoned and broken.

So he is for all of us who have known abandonment and brokenness. He accepts all who come his way.

Again and again, he invited us to his church to hear the good news: God loves us! Forgives us! And there's no far-country too far that God's not looking way down the road to welcome us home. "Amen!!!" Now that's really good news. There was testimony from Mr. Mackens' people of his being the Church—Christ in the world—where broken minds and bodies and spirits have been healed. "Praise the Lord!!!"

"In every nation any one who fears him and does what is right is acceptable…" The rub comes in doing what is right, and there are myriad interpretations of the "right" from East to West. The Orthodox seemed to find their "right" in awesome reverence, singing and chanting a liturgy handed down the ages. The Church of God of Prophecy seemed more a family with the Holy Spirit and babies speaking together, reminding us of our oneness. If God is truly the power of unconditional love, any person, any nation, any creed, and liturgy that lives out this love is acceptable.

Whoever the neighbor is, is cherished—never ridiculed, abandoned, declared useless, and certainly, never killed. Oh, that our nation can discern what is right. God knows no partiality. All are his children.

PRAISE THE LORD. AMEN.

Unorthodoxy and Questionable Theology

87

The wind blows where it wills, and you hear the sound of it, but you do not know whither it comes or whither it goes; so it is of every one who is born of the spirit.

Christ to Nicodemus—John 3

But the hour is coming, and now is, when the true worshiper will worship the Father in spirit and in truth, for such the Father seeks to worship him.

Christ to the woman of Samaria--John 4

In our Sunday school class a few weeks ago, we wrestled mightily with the Trinity, the Holy Ghost, in particular. The Holy Ghost won't turn me loose. It keeps haunting me. As a child my father told ghost stories that curdled my blood at every innocent tapping of twigs on the windows and at every hoot of the owl, that harbinger of death. His imitation of the death rattle of an old woman "who was all skin and bones" and who died at the church house door made me doubly afraid of the Holy Ghost that the preacher was ever entreating to fall on us. How could a ghost full of holes fall through the tongue and groove ceiling! There were plenty of red wasps who found their quarters there, and fell on us in the winter when they were warmed by the pot-bellied stove from their torpid state. But the holy ghost never fell.

Later in life I was invited to The True Pentecostal Holy Ghost Church of God in Christ where the Holy Ghost not only descended but slew all there—even the piano player—and left one lone wholly confused sinner upright. The spirit writhed them on the floor, caused them to speak in tongues, to awake and prophesy, and then return to the realm of the Holy Ghost. I crept out the back door before the ghost could catch me.

The unresolved ghosts of my old faith chase me yet. The creeds of our faith confound me—and they did the Church fathers who wrote them. Years were spent haggling over every phrase, trying to state the unknowable... "was incarnate by the Holy Ghost of the Virgin Mary..." How did this Holy Ghost cause conception? Was it sexual or stated in mythological language that was borrowed from the Greeks whose heroes always had supernatural births? I don't know. And my mother would not approve of my wondering. Bless her dear heart and may she forgive me for all my idle words that she said must be answered for in the hereafter.

The King James Version of the Bible and the Unrevised Prayer Book left lingering with the Holy Ghost until the wind of the Holy Spirit blew from realms I know not where. In our class, I declared that this part of the God Head, the Spirit, was the only part of this Three-headed God that is truly on my acquaintance list. I speak to the Spirit. He, she, or it speaks to me. God is everywhere, Christ is seated at his right hand, wherever that is, and he said that he must go away so the Comforter, the Spirit, might come. Two thirds of the head left the one third that I know. It comes from I know not where, but I feel its breath that bids me worship in Spirit and in Truth. The tongues of fire is sometime too hot and I extinguish it, or it burns with creative power, a source beyond my knowing. And will this spirit teach me all things? All that I know—small though it be—of the mystery and majesty of creation, the unfathomable wisdom of the Eternal, the providence that leads us through the maze of our earthly existence, the yearning for the final overcoming of evil by good, and of the revelation of the love that will not let us go has come from the burning of the Spirit. Even as I write these lines, this wind speaks through the beginning lines of this old hymn—"Breathe on me breath of God. Fill me with life anew. That I may love what Thou dost love and do what Thou wouldst do."

88

Gird up your loins like a man and I will question you, and you will declare to me. Will you even put me in the wrong? Will you condemn me that you may be justified?

God to Job. Job 40:7-8

The following account may be apocryphal, but my mother told it as she had heard it: In our rural congregation there was a misreading from the book of Job by a young man just "called to preach." He read thusly: "Grit up your lions like a man," and he took this reading for his sermon's text.

We in the Episcopal Church must both "grit our lions" and "gird our loins" as we face the most divisive issue of our times, the ordination of Bishop V. Gene Robinson, an openly practicing homosexual. My judgmental lions gritted as I read in the Prayer Book on the examination of bishops this question: "Will you guard the faith, unity, and discipline of the church?" and his answer, "I will for the love of God."

So we must gird our loins like redeemed children of God and answer some questions: Shall we put God in the wrong that we may be justified? Is there a new work of the spirit for absolute all-inclusiveness that we, in our limited knowledge cannot understand? Let us hear what the Rabbi Gamaliel proclaimed in the Book of Acts concerning the teaching about the risen Christ: "If this plan or this understanding is of men, it will fail; but if it is of God, you will not be able to overthrow it…In that case you may be found fighting against God."

In the past history of the Anglican Communion there have been hard questions and much girding of the loins and gritting of lions. During the American Revolution, the Anglican Church in the States was almost abandoned. Then there was North-South—the issue of slavery; the suffrage of women; the civil rights movement; the Prayer Book revision; the ordination of women; the inclusion of the gay community; and, at last, the hardest of all—the

Unorthodoxy and Questionable Theology

ordination of a sexually-active gay bishop of the Church. How the lions roar and the loins quiver! Where is the Spirit leading us? Will there be schism?

I agree with one thing President Bush has said: "We are all sinners." We have all broken our vows, been unfaithful to our spouses one way or another, refused to be honest before God. We, like Job, are so human, so finite, so lacking in understanding, so set in our iron-clad opinions that we must confess with him: "I know that thou canst do all things and that no purpose of thine can be thwarted—Therefore, I have uttered what I did not understand, things too wonderful for me, which I did not know…therefore I despise myself and repent in dust and ashes."

Being repentant, let us never forget we are forgiven sinners and the one law given us is to love one another, following the leading of the spirit, forever alive and renewing. This law of love includes all creation and everyone: street prostitutes, outcasts in all nation, Jews, Muslims, agnostics, heterosexuals, bisexual, whatever sexual, nasty neighbors, slime balls, all colors, preachers and politicians, rude drivers, Buddhists, Saddam Hussein, gay bishops and gritless lions and ungirded loins.

This is my favorite doxology in all the Bible—a promise that redeems all our messes and presents us through Christ's love "without blemish."

> *Now to him who is able to keep you from falling and to present you without blemish before the presence of his glory with rejoicing, to the only God, our Savior, through Jesus Christ our Lord, be glory, majesty, dominion and authority, before all time and now and forever, AMEN.*

> **Jude 24**

89

A man may be a heretic in the truth; and if he believes things only because his pastor says so, or the assembly so determines, without knowing other reason, though his belief be true, yet the very truth he holds becomes the heresy.

John Milton

I have written of Miss Glory Powers and her "True Eye", the eye to set you free. Now I mull and muse about another Great-Emancipator, Mr. Lewis Frances Strange, also late of Kirkwood. He was our mentor of broader ideas and wider horizons, one who challenged our self-righteousness and small-mindedness, not caring one Amen what the assembly determined. He laid my foundation for a "faith-to-live-by."

Mr. Strange we called him, and "strange" he was for our Kirk-in-the Woods, certainly strange in his uncommon dash of haberdashery and his delicious abandon of country orthodoxy. He was a Spanish-American War veteran, ramrod straight, exuding a military air, a rarity indeed in the environs of Guthrie, Kentucky. Whether he rode up San Juan Hill with the Rough Riders, I do not know; but he longed to return to the Caribbean and the light from other climes never left his eyes. Being a veteran gave Mr. Strange an impressive advantage: He had a pension. Now if you got any sort of "check" during the thirties, you were rich, and as we knew, riches often equated privilege—privilege to dress well and privilege to be your own man. Mr. Strange did both.

I can see him yet. He was thin, not tall, but he always wore a tall hat: a high panama in summer, a five-gallon felt in winter. Since my father, uncles, and most male Kirkwoodians had the indestructible blue serge suit, how well I remember the snap of Mr. Strange's pinstripe, replete with vest half-circled by a great golden chain and fob, ajingle with exotic coins from the Spanish Main, or perhaps from Long John Silver himself. What a tingling moment when he would suck in his breath, sigh, look out across the churchyard, and casually bring out a bejeweled watchcase and pop

Unorthodoxy and Questionable Theology

open its face. "It's time to highball," he would announce, which meant it was time to go home from meeting. Then the treasure returned to the pinstripe.

His eyes were small, dark, and scrutinizing. His voice was the same. He pierced you with his glittering eye and querulous voice and you leaned in with eye and ear. "What are you going to make of yourself?" was one of his stilettos which left us speechless but reminded me that Mr. Strange expected us to amount to something. At the time we couldn't imagine what, but I never forgot his expectations. He spent the majority of his "check" on his only son's education, valuing this legacy above all others.

But the time I remember Mr. Strange best was on the occasion of his being ordained Deacon at our church. He had been delayed for some years because of the suspicion of his unorthodoxy; but being "well-off" and the coffers needing his pocketbook, he was finally asked to sit for his examination. What an afternoon that was! Congregated were assorted preachers and hoary deacons who were invited to administer the doctrinal quiz. Mr. Strange was put in a chair facing two rows of these Grand Inquisitors. All the hair-splitting doctrines were dusted off, particularly the ones that separated us from the Methodists, the first being baptism by immersion: "Do you believe immersion is the only true form of Baptism?"

"I don't know about that." Always he prefaced his responses with his doubts. Then he added, "I never heard Christ making any noise about it one way or the other."

When the doctrine of "Closed Communion" came up, which meant that only members of that local church family could have the bread and wine, he vehemently didn't know about that. "You mean that if someone walked into your home that wasn't of your family you wouldn't ask them to have anything to eat? I was taught to welcome strangers. The Bible tells you to." (Silence from the jury.)

Finally the big question, the Calvinistic doctrine of predestination and the "security of the saved," not being able to "fall from grace,"

Unorthodoxy and Questionable Theology

came around. "I don't know about that." Skewering the judges with his piercing eye and his voice bitter with disgust, he added, "You preachers don't know either. You can read both ways in the Bible. You had better be studying about loving your neighbor and quit trying to teach fly specks. The Lord gave us two commandments—to love God and each other. That's all I need."

The Inquisitors were rather like the accusers of the woman taken in adultery. They ordained him and were gone.

Mr. Strange and my father were best friends and kindred souls. He always longed to go back to Cuba, and one day, late in his life, he said wistfully to my father, "Bracy, come go with me. On this trip we won't keep no books." He lived that way—not keeping any books but giving of his resources and wisdom and piercing our small beliefs with "I don't know about that."

Unorthodoxy and Questionable Theology

WARS

90

Gonna' lay down my burden, down by the riverside, down by the riverside; ain't gonna' study war no more.
Old Negro Spiritual

Weary and weighted, tired and worn, I ain't gonna stop studying wars that I know. It makes no sense; I don't understand. There is evil beyond my comprehension that has prevailed through the ages—since Cain slew Abel, since the sons of Abraham have fought over the same inheritance, since the religions of the world have bloodied the earth, since brother killed brother during our Civil War, since World Ward II took some of our nearest and dearest sons. With no respite, we have in Iraq today the continued hatred of the sons of Abraham. "There is no discharge in the war." Can't lay their burden down.

In the old photograph, circa 1919, Mr. Joe Killebrew is holding his grandson, Joseph Buckner Killebrew, son of Jack Killebrew and Emily Marshall Killebrew, late of Rossview. Little did Mr. Joe know of the fate of his beloved grandson. Flying a B-29, Joe went down with his crew over the Pacific and no trace of his plane was ever found. This was in 1944, near the end of the war. He left behind a wife and infant daughter whom he never held.

Joe was first cousin to my husband and living so close together, they were like brothers. Joe's death left a grief, unrequited, and a loss forever new. At Christmas, following Joe's disappearance in November, we, the neighborhood carolers, went to the Killebrew home. Through a window, we could see the father standing at the fireplace with his head bowed against the mantelpiece. He had a great burden to lay down, down by the Red River at Rossview.

Most thankfully, my only brother came home. He was trained as a Navy pilot for carriers and was on his way to the Pacific when the A-bomb was dropped. There has been great controversy over President Truman's decision, but after Iwo Jima and Okinawa's bloodbaths and the Japanese's absolute "no surrender" policy, he made his terrible choice. In President Truman's biography, he never wavered from his decision, never doubted a minute about the American lives saved. Maybe, my brother's? The great fleet, assembled for the invasion of Japan, came home. Another burden laid down.

One of my brother's closest friends did not come home. He lies, I understand, in some field in Normandy where he was buried with highest honors for courage beyond the call of duty. He was a medic tending the dying under heavy fire when he himself fell. "No greater love hath any man than to lay down his life for a friend." He was that sort of hero, a hero who knew his duty and died doing it.

My husband, having lived as a boy by a retired sea captain who told of his seagoing adventures, decided "to go down to the sea in ships." A little known fact is that the Merchant Marine had the highest mortality rate of any branch of the service. Their group has now been given full veteran's status. They were denied veteran's benefits after the war because of politics – distrust of unions. One could sign on the merchant fleet only through their unions. Read Richard Dana's "Two Years Before the Mast" and you will understand why a union was so necessary for these poor sailors, especially during sailing ship days.

Aboard the merchant fleet were "all sorts and conditions of men:" men who for physical reasons were rejected by the draft, men far too old for military service, and retired men who were in love with the sea. My husband rode with high-octane gas aboard across the North Atlantic. The man of Mars must have much gasoline, and in convoy the German subs were lethal. When the tankers were hit, there was no escape from the burning sea. Every supply – tanks, trucks, ammunition, guns, medical supplies, food, everything – crossed the Atlantic by ship. One Englishman commented that the Americans were going to sink England.

A great burden was lifted when the war ended and my future husband came home. Sixty years later, I still wrestle with this scourge of the nations, our wars and rumors of war, and our everlasting hatreds. My understanding is yet confounded. When and how do we lay down the burden of war?

Man in his humanity – a mixture of good and evil – cannot free himself. Christ told his apostles that there would always be wars and rumors of wars and "see that you are not alarmed." I should heed His voice. There is some great warfare beyond our knowing. St. Paul writes in Ephesians: "For we wrestle not against flesh and blood, but against principalities, against powers, against the rulers of darkness of this world, against spiritual wickedness in high places."

This struggle must declare that if man is ever loosed from these death angels of war, unshackled from these powers and principalities, it must be from a power beyond our knowing, by some intervention from the coming of a new kingdom. My burden I lay down in these hopes. "Ain't gonna' study war no more."

91

And when ye hear of wars and rumors of wars, be ye not troubled, for such things must needs be...
Mark 13

When I had seen Ken Burns' PBS series on the Civil War, these words of Christ "for such things must needs be" began to haunt my mulling and musings. These things must needs be! As a student of history, I long avoided the pages devoted to the Civil War. These accounts were too close, too personal, too irrational, too gory and certainly too painful, because as a child and even into the 30s and 40s, I was aware of the hot-eyed anger on both sides of my family. "Yankee" was still a dirty word. "Damn Yankee" was a Yankee who came South and stayed. If Abraham Lincoln had had horns and tail, he could not have been more vilified.

My grandmother Winn chilled our bones with the account of her father being taken in the middle of the night to show the Union

Forces the fording place in Red River at Port Royal; and she recounted—still with fear in her voice—how the soldiers cursed and threatened, leaving the family huddled in the dark until daybreak. Out in North Carolina, in the path of Gen. Sherman's march, Aunt Hattie told us in many anguished details of her home's destruction. Every piece of furniture was piled and burned, all china was broken (enough to make a path to the smokehouse after the war), the feather beds ripped open and emptied out the upstairs windows, all food in the pantry taken, the smokehouse emptied and, finally, all livestock driven away. Even though Aunt Hattie was a staunch Scotch Presbyterian, she had a hard time accepting her niece's marriage to a Presbyterian missionary. Why? He was from New York State.

On the other side of my family, it was another story: My mother's people lived on the south side of Cumberland River in Montgomery County; the planters and slave holders lived on the north side. This made all the difference. In the hills and hollows of Palmyra, there were no plantations and certainly no wealth. Grandma Wickham was a Unionist. When the Confederate conscriptionists came, she hid her sons in the rag barrels kept for carpet making; she willingly cooked for the Union soldiers who impressed her for a night's lodging; she was an Abolitionist, counseling relatives and neighbors; and when the Union was being restored, she was one of the first in the county to make a two-day trip by wagon to Hopkinsville to take the oath of Allegiance for readmittance to full citizenship in the Union.

So was the dichotomy of my childhood allegiance, giving me a background of understanding as I search in my final years for some glimmers into a more faithful allegiance, for "those things that must needs be."

It must be that "he had loosed the fateful lightning of his terrible swift sword." The PBS historians made this point. Without the resolution of the Civil War, we would have been a fragmented nation, slavery would probably have been entrenched even into the 20th century, and the liberty—imperfect though it is—that we proclaim never would have been heralded worldwide. The

Emancipation Proclamation yet reverberates. His truth is marching on in Russia, Eastern Europe, China, South Africa and in the longings of all nations. Being dragged, screaming through history, we are often too dull and too blind to see "His day is marching on."

I have strived to be the blessed peacemaker, have prayed for peace, protested for peace; but after World War I ("To Make the World Safe for Democracy") and World War II ("The War to End All Wars,") Korea and Vietnam to rid us of the Communists and finally—at the present moment, Iraq—my hope for peace in my time is dead. "I know that these things will be, man being as he is, and even must be," as Christ said. Surely the desolation of Iraq holds the promise of the "terrible swift sword."

J. Glenn Gray in his book, "The Warriors," attempts to fathom the mystery of why men go to war. He makes the point that it is recorded in Holy Scriptures in the Revelation of John that there was war in heaven causing the devil and his angels to be cast out upon the earth. There is some great warfare beyond our knowing, some struggle for righteousness that causes the nether region around us to seethe in its agony. St. Paul writes in Ephesians: "For we wrestle not against flesh and blood, but against principalities, against powers, against the rulers of darkness in this world, against spiritual wickedness in high places." This struggle must declare that if man is ever loosed from these death angels of war, unshackled from these powers and principalities, it must be by divine intervention, "beyond the human, in the nature of being itself," unto the coming of His kingdom.

> *He hath sounded forth the trumpet that shall never call retreat;*
> *He is sifting out the hearts of men before the judgment seat,*
> *Oh, be swift my soul to answer Him*
> *Be jubilant my feet!*
> *Our God is marching on.*
>
> **The Battle Hymn of the Republic**

www.ingramcontent.com/pod-product-compliance
Lightning Source LLC
Chambersburg PA
CBHW022111150426
43195CB00008B/352